Contact Your Angels

Now!

It's Easier Than You Think!

By Dawn Lianna MA

Copyright

Contact Your Angels Now!

It's Easier than You Think!

Author: Dawn Lianna M.A.
Publisher: Eagle Song Healing 2013

All rights reserved. No part of this book may be reproduced or transmitted in any form or by any means, electronic or mechanical, including photocopying, recording or by any information storage and retrieval system, without written permission from the author, except for the inclusion of brief quotations in a review.

Editing, credits and special thanks to: Kate O'Rielly, Adie Shaw, Jhorna Hochstedler, Ed Riddle, Beth Roche, Elaine VanGordon, Nancy Brown and Ron Holman.

Book cover by DesignerPassport.com

ISBN-10: 1490498273

Dedication

This book is dedicated to the Angels and to all of you wonderful Earth Angels out there doing such great work on the planet. I am grateful you are reading this, because I know you are an Angel too.

I give a very special thanks for all my students, teachers and friends who have guided me along the way. To my beloved Guides and Angels in the inner realms, I thank you with my whole heart.

May we all be blessed with peace on Earth.

With deepest love,

Dawn Lianna MA
Website: www.intuitivecallings.com
Phone: 503-699-3035
Email: dawn@dawnlianna.com

Foreword

From far past your imagination comes the energy of Angels. The Angels come from a place of love beyond our current perceptions.

As I move into this book, with curiosity, openness and love, I am amazed and blessed with what I find. Dawn Lianna has been connecting with Angels since childhood. In this book she shares how to make those connections!

Dawn is self-taught through direct experience and has an uncanny ability to transmit this skill. When you place your concerns, hopes and expectations, in your heart of hearts and connect with the Angels, there is help for you from beyond your current understanding.

So, buckle up boys and girls, mamas and papas, saints and sinners, as all are welcome here. In the land of the Angels we are all loved and blessed.

I have learned and caught many teachings from Dawn Lianna. Please take the time to do the same and "Contact Your Angels Now".

Ron Holman, PhD

Preface

While writing this book, I have been talking to the Angels frequently. I've invited them in, several times a day. As I have done so, my life has taken many amazing turns for the better in so many ways. It's proof that these processes really work.

I see the Angels even more frequently, walking in crowded rooms, on busy streets, in traffic and holding space for myself and others. I have had a personal quantum leap, that I didn't expect.

I find myself feeling wonderful, old patterns are changing more easily and I am happier and kinder to myself. I have always been one to count my blessings, and this has become so natural now. The love in my life has increased and I am so grateful.

Please join me in calling in the Angels to empower your life. Ask for what you want and need and allow for their blessings. Pray for others and for the Earth. Ask the Angels to bless us all! They are here to help us to change things for the better.

Love to you all,

Dawn Lianna MA

Table of Contents

    Introduction xii

Chapter One
    My Third Near Death Experience.......................1
        Much More to Learn Here 1

Chapter Two
    Getting to Know the Angels! 9
        My Own Childhood 9
        Set Your Intention & Dial in the Angels.....10
        Listen From Your Sweet Spot 11

Chapter Three
    Call Your Angels Now 15
        How This Book is Put Together 15
        Create an Angel Journal 16
        Be Present and Mindful..............................16
        How to Be Even More Mindful 17
        Sample Language to Call Your Angels.......20

Chapter Four
    Know Your Guardian Angels 23
        Exercise: Meet Your Guardian Angel 24
        When Elena Met Her Guardian Angel 26
        Becky's New Mom Angel Story 26
        Joyce's Story: Angels Do Exist 27
        A Loving Message from Your Angels 29
        Home Play 29
        A Loving Angel Message 30

Chapter Five
    How Do Angels Communicate? 31
        Use Your Senses to Know Your Angels.......31
        How Do Angels Communicate? 31

Your Potent Inner Senses 32
Clairvoyance: Your Inner Eyesight 32
Open Your Third Eye 33
Clairsentience: Your Inner Feelings 33
Clairaudience: Your Awesome Inner Ears.34
Claircognizance: Your Inner Knowing 36
Amazing Signs and Signals 36
A Powerful Sign From My Dad 36
Hannah Hears Her Angel –She's All Ears!.37
Sharing Jeanette's Story 40
Jeanette's Compelling Angel Miracle.........41
Exercise: Receive Your Angel's Name........41
A Message from the Angels 44
Home Play 44
A Loving Angel Message 45

Chapter Six
Your Angel's Gift & Sweet Heart 47
Angel Gifts 47
Gift Exchange with Your Guardian Angel .48
Connect to Your Angel's Heart 50
Exercise: Connect to Your Angel's Heart...50
Patty's Angel Gift Story 51
Sonia's Angel Heart Story 51
Michelle's Angel Gift Story 52
A Message from the Angels 52
Home Play 53
A Loving Message From the Angels...........54

Chapter Seven
Your Body Angel or Body Deva 55
Exercise: Get to Know Your Body Angel....56
Charlie's Body Angel Story 57

vii

The Overlighting Body Deva Angels 58
Exercise: Overlighting Body Angels 58
A Message from the Body Angels 59
Home Play 60
A Loving Angel Message 60

Chapter Eight
Get to Know the Archangels 61
Introducing Archangel Metatron 63
A Message from Archangel Metatron 65
Archangel Michael 65
An Experience with Archangel Michael 67
The Point of the Story 70
A Message from Archangel Michael 70
Archangel Gabriel 71
A Message from Archangel Gabriel 74
Archangel Raphael 74
Archangel Raphael Loves Children 75
A Message from Archangel Raphael 76
Archangel Chamuel and Team 76
Archangel Zadkiel and Team 77
Exercise: Get to Know the Archangels 78
Your Archangels' Message 79
Home Play 80
A Loving Message From Your Angels 81

Chapter Nine
Introducing The Matriarchal Angels 83
The Matriarch Angels 84
Matriarch Angel Team Muriel 85
Matriarch Angel Team Haniel 86
Matriarch Angel Team Terasita 87
A Message from Matriarch Angel Terasita 88

    Matriarch Angel Team Arial 89
Chapter Ten
    Get to Know the Special Task Angels 91
        Special Task or Project Angels 91
        The Money and Prosperity Angels 92
        Your Business Angels 93
        The Traveling and Traffic Angels 93
        Joyce's Late Night Road Angel Story 94
        Story: Angels Turn the Pallet in Mid Air ... 96
        Parking Angels 98
        Jo's Parking Angel Story 99
        Mother Angels 99
        Father Angels 99
        Creator and Clearing Angels 100
        Creator Angels 100
        Clearing Angels 100
        Planetary Angels 102
        Universal Angels 102
        Cherubs 103
        The Mighty Alohem 103
        Angels Who Walk Among Us 104
        Exercise: Special Task Angels 105
        A Traveler's Angel Story 106
        An Angel Message 107
        Home Play 108
        A Loving Angel Message 108
Chapter Eleven
    Angels of Hearth and Home 109
        The Angels of Your Own Home 109
        Exercise: Meet the Angels of Your Home . 110
        Sacred Spaces and Altars 112

    Use the Elements to Build an Altar 112
    Element 112
    Air Element 113
    Fire Element 113
    Water Element 113
    Yin/Yang 114
    Use the Feng Shui Bagua 114
    Invite in the Masters 115
    Keep it Simple 115
    Write a Love Letter to the Angels 116
    Jaxine's House Angel Story 116
    Jan's Altar Story 117
    A Message from the Angels about Altars ..117
    Home Play 118
    A Loving Message from the Angels...........119

Chapter Twelve
    Get to Know Other People's Angels 121
    Working with Other People's Angels 121
    Get to Know Other People's Angels..........122
    Kristen's Fascinating Angel Story 123
    Ann's Angel Story 124
    How to Talk to Children about Angels 124
    Annie's Miraculous Guardian Angel 125
    Emily's Childhood Angel Story 126
    Exercise: Know Someone Else's Angels ...127
    A Message from the Angels 127
    Home Play 128
    A Loving Angel Message 128

Chapter Thirteen
    The Healing and Comfort Angels....................131
    Working with the Sweet Healing Angels ..131

Angels of Comfort and Change 132
Grief and Loss..133
Angels and Coping with Death 134
The Keepers of Life and Death 135
Exercise: Healing and Comfort Angels 136
Ron's Story of His Mother's Passing 137
Alice's Empowering Angel Story 138
Carol's Touching Angel Story 138
Kate's Intense Angel Story 139
A Heartfelt Message from the Angels 141
Meet Your Angel's Review 142
An Enchanting Message from the Angels 142
Home Play 143

Chapter Fourteen

A Joyful Conclusion 145
A Blessing from Your Angels....................146
About The Author 147
Additional Resources................................148
Additional Books By Dawn Lianna, M.A. 149
Dawn's International Trainings 149
Contact Dawn Lianna, M.A. 150
Do You Have an Angel Story? 151

Introduction

The purpose of this book is to help you connect with your own pure intuition, your Spirit Guides and the magnificent Angels that surround you. The Angels wish to remind you of their deep, abiding love for you.

You can call on your Angels anytime, day or night and they will come. By calling them in, you increase their loving stewardship to help you with your precious life.

In these challenging times, many people write me with stories of both their hardships and joys. Some find their faith is thin and they don't understand why the Angels don't intervene to stop the destruction we see on Earth. We live in free will and the Angels can't overstep the boundaries of our dimension. Yet, as you call on them, YOU empower the Angels.

Others write of profound experiences of how their lives were touched by an Angel. I share many of those empowering and moving stories here.

When you see a message here that is in bold, italics and quotes, know that this is a message to you directly form the Angels. I feel privileged to be able to bring their sweet goodness through to you. I had so much fun writing with them.

Take your time and contact your Angels. Every precious moment you spend with them amplifies the goodwill in your life 1000 fold with blessings.

All my love,

Dawn Lianna, M.A.

Chapter One
My Third Near Death Experience

"When love comes knocking on the door of your heart or your life, open wide. Receive the blessing. Love what is and trust yourself. We are knocking on the door of your heart right now. Open wide and receive our love."

The Angels through Dawn Lianna

Much More to Learn Here

One of the most significant events of my life was my most recent near death experience. I've actually had three near death experiences. That truly means that three times during this lifetime, I have died, crossed over to the other side and come back.

My first near death experience was at birth. I don't remember that experience very well. I know that I was reluctant to come into this lifetime and that my little, newborn body had a hard time adjusting to this world. As I got closer and closer to coming in, I realized what I was coming into and I wished I could change my mind!

My second near death experience was at age 6, when I was sick for about six months. I was actually hospitalized for having measels, mumps and pneumonia all at the same time, scaring my parents and caregivers half to death themselves! I remember bits and pieces of that journey home, but I don't remember the whole experience consciously.

My third near death experience was in December of 1992, which I remember as vividly, as if it was yesterday. I tell the story in full elsewhere but I want to gift you here with part of the experience, which was and still is truly Angelic.

I was living in Arcata, California with my then husband and our son, who was at that time 12 years old. I often light a candle in the morning for meditation, and that day I forgot to blow out the candle, as I dashed off to work.

When I got home the house was on fire. I called the fire department, but they didn't show up. I tried to put the fire out myself and ended up inhaling a lot of smoke.

The house was gutted by the fire, with the structure still standing. We were displaced from our home for two months after the fire and stayed in a hotel nearby, during that time.

While staying in the hotel room, I got a very bad case of pneumonia. One afternoon, I was having immense trouble breathing. I was literally gasping for air. My lungs were closing up. Remembering that a hot steaming bath worked well for colic with a baby, I climbed into a hot bath, inhaling the steam. I could hardly breathe. I was choking and gasping for air but none would come. I remember taking my last breath and letting go.

I traveled through a very dark tunnel wondering where I was, when looking ahead I could see a pin hole of light in the distance. I realized I was in the tunnel.

I burst through the end of the tunnel into the most amazing light. The re was a blissful feeling of love stronger than anything I had remembered experiencing before, though it was very familiar. The love was palatable everywhere.

I spent 45 minutes over there visiting in the light. I didn't spend time with my relatives, I wanted to go straight to source, and I did. I bathed in a love that is unfathomable to me now. My faith in a divine Power is unshakable about that amazing visit with the profound Light of Love.

When that was complete, I began to consciously travel backwards at the speed of light, returning toward Earth. Until the second, I began to return, I had no awareness that I'd be coming back here. I was home.

I shot back into my body making the loudest sound I have ever heard. It was as if a giant clap of thunder happened between my ears and inside my body, mind, heart and soul. That sound seeming to bring my being and my body back to life.

I sat up and caught my breath. The water in the tub and my body were very cold. I had been gone awhile. My body started to shiver.

I looked up. Right there, right by my bathtub, were two giant Angels. They were standing in the room next to the tub with me. My jaw dropped. This was not a vision of two Angels. This was a physical manifestation of the two Angels. They were as present in the room as I was. There was no veil between us.

There giant wings swooped to the ceiling, tall, arched and exciting to see. I recognized them as Archangels. When I asked in amazement, "Who are you?" they answered, right out loud in voices made of love. The first one said, "I'm Michael" and the other said, "I'm Gabriel." I was so touched and amazed, I almost started crying.

Michael said, "We brought you back. It is time to get out of the bathtub." They literally helped me get out of the tub and wrapped me in a towel. They told me to lie down and someone would be coming to the door in one half hour.

As I laid down, the Angels said, " We will be with you for three days. We will guide you back to health. Please follow our instructions precisely."

For three days, they stayed. They gave me instructions on what to do, told me stories about many things, and gave me a lot of instructions about my life. I followed their instructions to the detail and over the next three days, my little body quickly returned to a state of robust health.

I didn't know until months later that my guests and family members didn't see the Angels there. I spoke their instructions and folks waited on me hand and foot as if they heard them too. I watched people walk around them and sit on another part of the bed or a chair nearby but not once did someone try to sit where those Angels were sitting.

I spent those three days with those beautiful Angels totally present in bliss. I remember many things they taught me and I absorbed many stories so deeply, that I can't remember them consciously.

The experience opened me up in a whole new way.

I was filled with a sense of underlying purpose and I knew that my purpose would happen without my doing much. It was not up to me. It was naturally fulfilled.

At the end of the third day, Archangels Michael and Gabriel told me it was time for them to leave. They said that when they left, I wouldn't see them in the same way anymore, but that they would always be with me. They said that anytime I wanted, I could talk to them and they would always respond. They told me I shouldn't be concerned when my awareness of them changed.

I thanked them deeply without any thought of loss and they graciously disappeared out of my physical sight. I could still sense their presence but not in the same clear way. It was then, like it is now. I can feel them and see them, while I am writing this story for you, but they are a bit vague, wispy and not in full-blown 3-D, like they were at that time. I continue to communicate with them as often as possible.

I still feel especially close to those Angels. Any slight doubt of their existence was completely erased. I know they are here all the time.

I tell you this story to start, because most of us wonder if this stuff of the angels is real. We sense it in a vague way and even though it is profound, it is usually not a physical plane experience, so we have that sense of wonder about it.

After this amazing experience in 3-D, I can't doubt it anymore. I have tried to conjure up doubt. I can't. I have had people tell me they don't believe me, but my experience is as real to me as the rest of my daily life living memories. I am certain of my own experience. So I am here to testify to their very real existence.

My daily experiences with them now, is much more subtle. I'm happy to recieve a whisper from the, or a whispful experience of them brushing past me. I'm so excited when I see them ministering in crowds, to those who need attention. I'm so happy to be chosen by them to bring this work forward to you.

Chapter Two
Getting to Know the Angels!

Your Angels are excited that you are interested in contacting them. I know because they told me so. They are so ready to connect with you. They take great joy when anyone wants to build a relationship with them. Know that they are celebrating.

I am also excited to embark on this journey with you and the Angels. I will share with you some of the many profound experiences I've had with Angels. I will also share with you, many stories that I've been by students and friends of their own experiences with the Angels. I'll share some meditations and exercises to help you, and I'll share some Angel messages.

My Own Childhood

My early childhood was extremely challenging. I grew up in a home where there was a profound mix of love and abuse, and a deep denial that this abuse existed. At that time I took refuge with the Angels. Like many of you, I wondered many times why I had to go through such challenges.

I've spent many years recovering from childhood, gathering my life force and recovering my soul.

Without the Angels help, I doubt if I would have survived at all. Through some profound events, I developed an undeniable connection to them and came out whole! It's truly a miracle, and at the same time, it sure hasn't been easy. The Angels have protected me through thick and thin, and kept me alive. I love them dearly.

I kept my gifts to myself most of my life. Now in this amazing time, I'm free to shar these gifts and experiences with you. I hope that it will help you to connect with them more deeply and believe in your experiences even more.

I know that some of you have also had profound and subtle experiences with the Angels, and some of you are still waiting and hoping to connect with them. I trust that with the help of these tools you will be able to deepen your connection.

I pulled a lot of tools from the field of Neuro-Linguistic Programming (NLP). I also learned directly from the Angels, how to help you connect and celebrate with them. I will teach you those tools here.

Set Your Intention & Dial in the Angels

It does not matter if you have ever connected with your Angels before. Your pure desire and intention to call them in and connect with them is enough. Learning to hear, see and feel the presence of Angels is a gift and yet it does take time to develop your intuitive skills. Your awareness can continue to grow for the rest of your sweet life.

Some people sense their Angels very easily and others do not. Most importantly, accept what is and what you do get. If you allow yourself to get frustrated over your progress, that can slow down your connection.

Don't compare your skills to anyone else's skills. We each have amazing talents and strong suits. You can learn to connect more deeply just as I and countless others have done. Your experiences will be unique and unlike anyone else's experience. Remember, it is equally valid.

Listen From Your Sweet Spot

Angels are quiet beings, so it's important to quiet your mind when you are tuning in and listen from your sweet spot. That is the quiet, peaceful place in your mind and heart.

I pretend my mind is as quiet as a stone, and center myself in my heart by breathing into my heart area. Then I call my Angels. I say, "Angels please come in close, so I can connect with you." Then I listen for their whispers, feel for the light touch of a feather and look for a very subtle change in the atmosphere. They come in on wings of light. Ssssh! Be really still.

Angels come simply because you ask for them. Ask them and they come. Sometimes they give me the chills, and other times when I'm feeling really distracted, sad or lonely, it's harder to hear and feel them. I may get a subtle feeling that I need to go to a special place in nature, like the beach, the river or the forest. Getting out helps me get quiet enough to feel and listen again. Daily meditative practices are key.

They will also show up pronto when you have a need. Sometimes I just say, *"Angels, Angels, please come in. I need your help now. Thank you."* They show up in a second when you ask and they help you nurse your deepest wounds until you feel better. Know that even, if you can't see them, they are there.

Some people think that Angels only in times of crisis. Yet, Angels are here all the time. Angels congregate in droves where people are happy and celebrating and doing meditative and spiritual activites. I also see them at hospitals, grocery stores, schools, crowded marketplaces and coffee shops. They are here among us all the time, helping as much as their stewardship will allow. It takes only a subtle shift in awareness and a bit of faith, to become aware of them.

Chapter Three
Call Your Angels Now

How This Book is Put Together

This book has eight chapters. Each chapter provides you with new information, an exercise to do, a real life, true Angel story and a special message for you from the Angels.

It's okay to just open this book and read. Yet I'd encourage you to also read from beginning to end. Each section builds on the one before it. We start with some basics on how to connect with the Angels and move forward from there. Then we discuss many different kinds of Angels and how they can help you in your life.

The final chapter will include even more empowering stories, original techniques and a great review of what you have learned.

The Angels are right here working with me and helping me write. They are there with you now as you read and learn. They are so happy to help. When you consciously invite them in, it increases their stewardship to help you and it gives them great joy.

Angels have many creative ways to communicate. They will get your attention any way they can. They flutter, smile, shift the energy, speak, touch, intend, and send thoughts, downloads, feelings, sounds, pictures, tastes and smells. They use all your inner senses, which we will discuss in full. When you notice something, it's time for a heads up.

Create an Angel Journal

I would love for you to start a paper or electronic journal to document your experiences as you read through the book. Take notes as you go and document the results of the exercises as you do them. People often tell me that their progress is gradual and if they had not documented it, they might not have realized how far they had come. It could start out mundane but it's about to get lively.

Because the Angels live in subtle dimensions, these kinds of changes are sometimes profound and sometimes very subtle. Please chart them. You will be glad you did.

Be Present and Mindful

Being present in your physical body is a very important part of being able to connect with the

Angelic realm. Some people mistakenly think they have to be able to space out to some far away Angelic dimension. This first exercise will teach you how to be present and prepared to contact your Angels.

Feel free to use your imagination and intuition, as they are twin flames. If you already practice grounding and I hope you do, please try it this way as well as use your own style.

How to Be Even More Mindful

1. Sit down and put your feet flat on the floor. Feel into the *"souls"* of your feet. Take some deep breaths and center yourself in your heart.

2. Place your attention on the bottoms of your feet. Imagine that you are growing roots from each of your feet. Send these roots down into the Earth below you, grounding yourself. Your roots can go clear to the heart of the earth to her magnetic core, and they only need to go a little ways to connect to the light of the Earth. As soon as they break through the crust or surface of the Earth, they land in her light of love.

3. Next, imagine a third root extending from the base of your spine, from your first

chakra. This root goes down into the Earth as well. This creates a tripod of light or roots underneath you. It's sort of like a three-legged stool, stable and strong.

4. Imagine that the Earth is full of bright light, as if there is a brilliant Sun inside her. Direct your roots right into that light. Pull the Earth's light up through your roots into your heart, filling yourself with light.

5. Imagine a brilliant Sun over the top of your head. This Sun represents the source of love in the Universe. Allow your crown (the top of your head) to reach up into that Sun, and tuck into it like a funnel. Allow the light of the Universe to come in through the top of your head and mix with the light of the Earth in your heart. Let it also fill up your aura with Sunlight. Bask in that for a moment or two. Feel your light increasing and glowing. Imagine it warm, loving and comfortably full.

6. Now pretend you can see your aura. Imagine it extends three feet from your body in a full circle around you. Then send your aura upward and tuck your whole aura into the Sun above you.

7. Next, extend your aura downward and tuck it into the Sun in the Earth below you. This creates a protective column of light around you.//
8. It reminds me of the "Beam me up Scotty" tube of light on Star Trek. It's awesome. This tube of light is very protective. It can be used every day all day long. It is safe to practice and use with children, people who are sick or the elderly.
9. Now ask your Angels to come in nice and close and stand right next to you. Give them permission to lean right into your aura and protect you. Ask them to stay with you throughout the day and night. I often ask for 10,000 Angels to be with me at all times. They love to come so why not?

Know that your Angels hear you. You may or may not yet be aware of their presence, but they are listening. Assume they have heard you and will do what you ask, because they do and they will.

I ground and anchor myself throughout the day. I want you to practice that, too. The more anchored you are, the easier it is to know your Angels. Stay grounded as you go to the next step, and practice getting to know your Angels now.

Sample Language to Call Your Angels

I want to give you some simple examples of ways to call in your Angels. Remember, you can call them anytime, for any reason. You want them to be with you in your daily life.

Here are some examples of statements, that you can use to call on your Angels. They are kin to affirmations and prayers. This may seem really obvious and simple to some of you, and that's great.

Many people have asked me how to call them in, so I want to be sure to share how I do it. Feel free to use these words or make up your own:

"Angels, please be with me. I call to this situation the highest and best energy. I ask my Guardian Angels to guide and guard me. I call upon the Angels to help everyone involved in this situation for the highest possible outcomes."

"Beloved Guardian Angels please come to my awareness. I trust that you are here and I would like to know you better. I am grateful for your service. Please help me to get to know you now."

"Angels, please come in. I need you right now. Thank you."

After you request your Angels to come, tune in and let go. Allow your energy to become soft. Shift to your peripheral vision. Quiet your mind and heart and watch for subtle cues. Take some time right now and call your Angels to you.

"When you are in need, we are here with you. Turn your worries and cares over to us. Ask us to help you unload the pain in your heart and of your world. We are right here ready to help. We love you. If you don't ask, we cannot interfere. If you have a longing in your heart, ask us to mellow that longing and turn it to satisfaction with what is. When you accept what is, even more good can come."

The Angels through Dawn Lianna

Chapter Four
Know Your Guardian Angels

Each of us has at least one personal Guardian Angel. Your Angel loves you more than you can imagine. Consider how a most loving mother cherishes her child, and then multiply that by millions. They told me that is how much they love us.

Some of us have more than one Guardian Angel. In a certain way, we all have many Angels helping us. I am referring now to your personal Guardian Angel who stands right behind you, like you have seen in the pictures. There is a reason why many artists have drawn them hovering over us in protective stances. They are often in that posture.

Your Guardian Angel may have been with you much of, or all of your life. Some people have the same Angel for an entire lifetime, while others may experience a shift of Angelic helpers or additional helpers in challenging times. Consider yourself lucky to have one Angel and, of course, extra lucky when you have more than one. We each have all that we need.

The purpose of your Guardian Angel is to guide and protect you. Your Angel knows your destiny, your purpose and helps to keep you on your path and out of harm's way. He or she gently nudges you in the right direction. Your job is to learn to sense the guidance and follow through on it.

Your Angel can't interfere with your soul contract or your free will, so please ask for help frequently. Your soul contract consists of the agreements that you, as your soul, made before you incarnated into this lifetime. Your contract includes the things you came to learn and clear, and the things you came to teach.

Your Guardian Angels are part of a bigger clan of Angels called protector Angels. There are multitudes of protective Angels to help you. Call on your Guardian Angels and the protector Angels when you feel the need for protection and direction.

Now we are going to take a journey and meet your Guardian Angel. Please get your Angel journal ready so you can take notes.

Exercise: Meet Your Guardian Angel

1. Ground and center yourself. Fill your aura up with light, like I showed you earlier.
2. Take some deep refreshing breaths and move into a state of relaxation.

3. Acknowledge your Guardian Angel. Tell your Angel that you want to meet him or her. Know that your Angel hears you whether you are aware of the Angel or not. Your Angel is probably standing right behind you.

4. Invite your Angel to come around in front of you. Know that when you invite your Angel to move, he or she will come around in front.

5. Sit quietly and listen for a moment. Simply watch, listen and feel for your Angel. There may be more than one.

6. Ask your Angels to ruffle their feathers, make some noise, and enter your reality in some way. Spend a few moments attuning.

7. Whether you receive anything consciously or not, know that your Angel hears you and is doing what you ask. Your Angel is very happy to be acknowledged and can hear and sense the words you are saying and the requests you are making, internally or out loud.

8. When you feel complete, ask your Angel to move back to his or her usual position behind you. Pay close attention as they move around you. Many people have had a

first contact with their Angels when they asked them to change positions and move around their auric field.

9. Thank your Angels deeply. Take some notes in your Angel journal and write down any insights, hints or images that you received. Pay attention to your dreams. Use all your senses.

When Elena Met Her Guardian Angel

"My Guardian Angel stands behind me. When I meditate I feel her but I rarely see her. She feels lovely, like I'm home.

The experience I had when I asked my Angel to come around in front and face me was quite a surprise. As I allowed myself to look, I saw she was very tall and slender with flowing robes, and wings that were velvety and large.

She radiated waves of love to me. She is a dark purple Angel. She helps protect the children beneath her wings and within her robes. She is amazing and I am honored to have her as my own Guardian Angel."

Becky's New Mom Angel Story

"Using intuition and telepathy with my team of

Angels and Guides has been a huge help with our new baby. When he starts crying, I quickly ask if he's hungry, gassy, or tired. I quickly get telepathic answers back in my head, which always seem right when I act on them. I call in our Archangels and the baby's Guardian Angel to help me."

Joyce's Story: Angels Do Exist

"I grew up with stories of Angels as a part of our culture. I was fascinated with Angels. I read as many books on Angels as I could. I often pondered whether they really existed, or if they were only mythical stories passed down through the ages.

I grew up in a family where children were seen but not heard, so I kept my vast inner searching and questioning to myself. It was many years later as a young married woman, with young children to raise, that I was to have an experience that proved to me, that indeed, Angels do exist.

When I was a little girl, I would get scared at night. I might awaken seeing a shadow in my closet, or have a bad dream of being chased or falling. Later, I had anxiety dreams when I had to recite a poem in school or take an important test.

Very early in my childhood, I developed a habit of 'rocking' back and forth with my eyes closed and humming the childhood nursery song, "A tisket a tasket, a green and yellow basket," The rocking and humming pushed away the fear and anxiousness. Soon I would drift off to sleep.

Years later at age thirty-six, my husband left me. I had been out of the work world for sixteen years and my sons were now teenagers. I felt shock, pain, and extreme fear for months. Though I had always been a deep sleeper, I was waking up in the middle of the night experiencing fear and anxiety. I worried about what to do and how to support myself and the boys.

I tried everything to get through the night. Up to that point in my life, I had managed to get through other life challenges and still sleep through the night. The lack of sleep was taking its toll.

One night I awoke with a strong feeling of doom and gloom. I commenced my childhood mantra. Out of the blue, I felt what seemed like a great hand resting firmly on my shoulder.

I was afraid to look. I buried my head under the covers still rocking and humming, but the great hand's warmth, strength and comfort remained. In my heart, I knew it was an Angel. A great calm and an amazing, delicious peace swept over me. I fell instantly into a deep sleep. I awoke in the morning feeling better, more refreshed than I had in months.

Though my struggles continued, I never again awoke in the middle of the night feeling distressed. My sleep was sound. I truly believe an Angel had been sent from on high to release me."

A Loving Message from Your Angels

"We send you great love. We are very happy you are taking this journey. We bless you and look forward to an ongoing connection with you. Remember, we are with you at all times. We have always been with you. Sometimes you are able to sense us. We hope to connect with you more consciously now. We are always here. No matter what is going on in your life, we love you.

The more you pay attention to us, the deeper and stronger our connection becomes. We are deeply happy to be of service to you. We too benefit by our contact with you. Through you, we are better able to serve humanity."

The Angels through Dawn Lianna

Home Play

1. Practice grounding and calling in your Guardian Angel, at least once a day.

2. Use the techniques to help you. I want to be conscious of my Angels all day long, don't you? Increase your intention to bring them in closely.
3. Please make notes about your experiences in your Angel journal.

A Loving Angel Message

"The dreams that have not manifested yet are the dreams of your future. Look at what you have right now. You have dreamed that up through your heart, thoughts, feelings and love. Look at all the good in your life and give thanks. Give thanks. Give thanks. Give thanks. If it seems like you are lacking in some way, find the place that is not. Changing your emotions and creating from a place of empowerment will change what is manifesting."

The Angels through Dawn Lianna

Chapter Five
How Do Angels Communicate?

Use Your Senses to Know Your Angels

I hope you are practicing the grounding exercise and calling your Angels daily. The more you practice, the better.

Ground now and call your Angels. Ask them to help you be fully present while you read. Get out your Angel journal and let's talk about how Angels communicate.

How Do Angels Communicate?

Your Angels communicate to you primarily through your inner senses. They also use boosts of knowing, telepathy, signs, signals, dreams, other people and animals.

They also sing. I've been blessed to hear the Angels sing Hallelujah a few times. Listen for octaves of sounds like Aah, Eeh, Ooh, Laa Laa and Hallelujah. It can sound like millions of Angels are singing Hallelujah. It's magnificent and brings tears of joy streaming down my face every time it happens.

Your Potent Inner Senses

Each of your senses: sight, sound, feeling, taste and smell has an inner and an outer part. You know your external senses very well. Your inner circuitry is familiar. On the inner, you see things in your mind's eye. You hear sounds and messages through your auditory circuitry. You taste, smell and feel things intuitively. Your intuition, Guides and Angels all use these same pathways to connect with you.

Clairvoyance: Your Inner Eyesight

Your inner eye (third eye) sees in the subtle dimensions. This is called Clairvoyance. Sometimes a person's inner eye opens quickly, but usually it is a more gradual process.

Imagine your inner eye has been sleeping during a wonderful, sweet, long nap, dreaming about Angels. As you open your inner eye, imagine waking up to the really pleasant and beautiful inner world where Angels abound.

Ask your Angels to come and stand around you right now. Soften your vision and use your inner eye to look for them. You can do this with your physical eyes open or closed. If you have your eyes open, shift to your peripheral vision. Ask to see them now.

Sit quietly for a few minutes looking and practicing before you move on. Breathe deeply and relax for awhile. When you are complete, take some notes in your journal.

Open Your Third Eye

Your third eye is buoyant. I sometimes imagine that it's as flexible as a ping-pong ball in a bowl of water. If you can imagine a ping-pong ball in water, then imagine it floating and being able to turn in every direction. When you see your third eye this way, it helps it to be more open and flexible.

Your inner eye does not see quite like your outer eyes. The images are something vivid and other times fast and fleeting. They might remind you of dreaming.

Clairsentience: Your Inner Feelings

It's fair to say that most of us are connected to our feelings. You know the difference between an external feeling, such as temperature or texture, and an inner feeling, such as grief or love. The ability to feel things deeply is called

Clairsentience. Feeling another person's feelings is called empathy.

You might receive feelings from the Angels in any part of your body. You may notice feelings in your whole body, your mid-line, your heart, your hands, feet or anywhere.

Notice the Angels again, now, and sense them with your feelings. Ask them to move around and flutter. Feel for movement. Even the slightest sensation is evidence of your connection. Spend a few minutes feeling them before you move on.

Take notes in your journal.

Clairaudience: Your Awesome Inner Ears

Your inner ears hear in the subtle dimensions. Perhaps you have heard a voice that guided you, or a tone, gong or something else that thundered or moved quietly through your mind. What sounds have you heard on the inner?

Imagine listening for the sound of a train that is very far away. Maybe this train comes at 3 a.m., every night and blows its whistle, but it hasn't arrived yet. You love the train's whistle and you notice that it is one minute before 3 a.m.

You open deep inside, quiet your mind and listen, waiting for the sound of the train. You become very still, waiting and expecting.

Or imagine you are a new parent and you have a newborn baby sleeping in a crib near you. You are dozing off to sleep, but a part of you is listening to the sounds the baby is making, expectant that at some point the baby will awaken and cry with hunger.

Now let's open to hearing your Angels. Be full of anticipation for your Angels, as you would be for that train or the sound of your newborn sleeping. You are expecting to hear them. This state of expectancy helps you to hear. Expect to hear the Angels.

The sounds from your Angels are as subtle as a feather dropping or a breeze. Ask your Angels to move around again, and this time to speak to you. You are listening for incredibly subtle sounds. Sit for a moment and be extremely still, listening.

Some people actually hear Angels in their physical ears. Most of us hear them subtly or telepathically. Practice listening with your right ear, then your left ear and then listen with both ears. Next, listen with your heart. What do you hear? Take some notes.

Claircognizance: Your Inner Knowing

Claircognizance is your gift of clear inner knowing. Remember a time when you knew that something was true, no one could talk you out of it, and you were correct. That is claircognizance.

Amazing Signs and Signals

Your Angels send you clues, signs and signals. They use billboards, friends, strangers, animals, dreams, music, surprises, synchronicity, connections and missed connections, phone calls, radio, internet, TV shows, clouds and other means to get your attention.

Be watchful throughout the day. You can also ask for signs. Be open to noticing signals and synchronicity and trusting them.

A Powerful Sign From My Dad

I had a significant experience recently that I'd love to share with you. My dad passed away years ago and I was missing him. It was my dad's birthday, March 3rd, and I asked my Angels to give me a sign from my dad.

I was riding as a passenger in a car and I saw a billboard that said, "Your father wants to talk to you!" That really caught my attention. Then I saw a second billboard right away and it said, "Dianna is a gem." Well, that is close enough to my last name that I was stoked. It was clear to me that was a message from my dad sent at my request from the Angels, and it sure felt wonderful.

Hannah Hears Her Angel –She's All Ears!

"I had recently bought a new pendulum, a beautiful deep blue lapis with a diamond moonstone on the front. Each day, for about a week, I would take it out and ask my usual yes or no questions. I found this frustrating though, because I wanted more.

Last night, I did used my pendulum again. This time when I asked my question and instead of seeing the pendulum swing, I heard a beautiful, crystal clear, female voice.

Her voice came in fast, clear and strong. My thoughts didn't have time to catch up with her. The voice was so loud and clear, I felt shocked. When I thought of a question, the answers came almost simultaneously. When I couldn't understand one of the words, she repeated it again.

The most important message I remembered hearing was; "We come in through the light you are offering".

To me, this means the only way we can hear them is if we allow ourselves to find the feeling space that matches, or is in the vicinity of what we are wanting. That doesn't mean we won't receive information unless we are happy. Being in a happy and trusting feeling enhances our connection.

Sometimes, I feel like I am blindfolded and cannot see; yet I choose to step forward anyway. A larger part of me knows it is all ok. There is a gigantic, gleaming, glowing pile of magnificent beautiful beings waiting for us to breathe, let go, jump in, take that step and open our hearts enough to allow all this love in.

I managed to hold the feeling or vibrational space of letting go, with all of my being, for just a little bit. I allowed the doors of my heart to fling open, and a flood of the purist most loving words, thoughts and feelings came through quicker and clearer than ever before.

The conversation I had with my Angels lasted for about 10 to 15 minutes. They were talking with me as if I was right there with them. I felt so much love and so much truth I was crying with joy and relief.

I clearly remember asking them for help because this had been one of the hardest weeks I'd experienced for a long time. I found it odd that I was able to hear them despite my inner turmoil.

I had never experienced light or love of this magnitude before. The pain was just that I was not keeping up with all that my life had brought forward to me. My attention had been on things that were not consistent with the truth of who I really was or am today.

Sometimes it takes a little bit of time for me to adjust to higher frequencies. At first it feels slightly uncomfortable. My fear comes up and I am unable to hold the frequency consistently. Yet, the larger part of me is coaching me and leading me forward.

So through my moment of just breathing and allowing, not pushing against anything, I let this new light of a higher potency rush through, which I now have with me forever more.

This is only the beginning of what is to come. With every experience we gain more insight, and a greater pool of light that is never ending in its expansion. Follow what feels easy and good in your heart.

We all receive information in unique ways; there are more ways to receive than we have words in our language to describe for them.

I feel like I receive information in a way that cannot be put into one category and we all have this ability. We were born with it, it is our true nature. Now the fun is re-remembering who we really are. Play with it; try the "make-believe" game you used to play when you were little. It is that easy, and should be that fun."

As you can see, Hannah had a very vivid experience with her Angels.

Sharing Jeanette's Story

I wanted to share this story with you from my friend Jeanette. Jeanette expressed that she was feeling frustrated with her intuition and especially in connecting with her Angels. She longed to get a message from them. The Angels sent their love to her in a unique way, letting her know that they were with her and hearing her. Your Angels and Guides are there with you too. They are ready, waiting and excited to work with you. This story speaks mountains to the fact that they are aware of our thoughts and good intentions.

Jeanette's Compelling Angel Miracle

"During an evening intuition class, I was not able to access my Angel the way that I wanted to. I was feeling frustrated and asked my Angels for a sign. I know that frustration gets in the way, yet I was having trouble.

The next day I experienced what I thought was a miracle. I was driving, when a phone call came in from my former work place. Several thoughts ran through my head as to why they were calling, sadly none of them positive. I chose not to answer the call and waited for the voice mail. The surprise message was from a former colleague. She wanted to know what I wanted to do with the Angel that was still at my desk.

How synchronistic that the call about the "Angel at my desk" would come at such a time that I felt forsaken because I didn't have the experience I wanted. I know my Angel is with me. Right now, he shows himself in other ways. I will be patient."

Exercise: Receive Your Angel's Name

Now let's connect with your Guardian Angel more deeply and open up to receiving his or her name.

Pay close attention to each of your senses and open to receive information in every possible way. Remember to take notes.

1. Ground and center yourself. Fill up with light.

2. Ask your Guardian Angels to move around to the front of you.

3. Use your inner eyes to see your Angel. Use your peripheral vision.

4. Next shift your attention to your feelings. Ask your Angels to keep moving around, and feel any subtle sensations.

5. Next, open up your listening skills. Ask them to speak, sing, and play their trumpets. Request right out loud that they show up for you. Ask them to celebrate and make some noise. Listen for those sounds.

6. Shift to sensing the Angels with your nose and mouth. Smell and taste the Angels.. What do these senses tell you?

7. Now, open all your senses together and play with your Angels. Remember, if you get a little bit, a lot, or seemingly no information consciously, you did connect with your Angels. Give them your thanks. Continue shifting back and forth between

8. Quiet your mind again and listen deeply. Ask for your Angel's name. Receive your impressions. The range of names is wider than you have ever heard. They may come in your native tongue, a spiritual language, or as a vibration or tone. They can be as simple as the names Anna, Michael or Joe, or as elaborate as Claire Anastasia or Amanita Rose. Be open. Write down any names or insights you receive.

- Sometimes people hear the name on the first try and other times it takes a few attempts. Sometimes it helps to sound syllables out loud. I did that with a client today. Her Angel's name had a long Aaaaah sound, but I couldn't quite get the name. So I started sounding, "aaaaah." Then came "naaaaaaa", then "mmmaaaa." I then put it together and it was the name, Annama. That was a name I had not heard before, and it is so beautiful.

As you practice this exercise, you are opening each of the subtle senses. Use this exercise if you are very advanced or just beginning. Practicing increases your connection. I am doing it right now and I am seeing three beautiful Guardians moving around me.

A Message from the Angels

"Whether you see us or not, we are here. We are right here among you every day. Your very intention to connect with us gives us great joy. Can you feel that joy right now? We love you as much as life itself. We are really joyous that you are tuning in.

Each of you has at least one subtle sense that is already prominent for you. You lean into this sense every day. Are you a feeler? Are you a person who gets a lot of inner pictures? Do you spend time listening on the inner? Do you have a strong sense of inner knowing?

Pay great attention to your inner sense that is the most developed. We will work with you right now through that sense. Use it now to sense our presence with you. We remind you that we are here and you are loved."

The Angels through Dawn Lianna

Home Play

1. Call your Angels in every day and spend at least ten minutes connecting. Imagine your

inner senses are wide open. Practice listening, feeling, watching, tasting and smelling for them. Continue to invite them to come in front of you. The key is to open all of your senses. Be open to telepathy. Be playful. Remember, they love you no matter what.

2. If you have received your Angel's name begin to use it. If you have not yet received your Angel's name, continue to ask for it. Pay attention. Your instincts are correct. If you have been thinking of a name or dreamed of a name, trust what you get.

3. Please document your experiences in your Angel journal.

A Loving Angel Message

"You are love. You are magnificent. Be grateful for your gifts. It won't bounce your ego off the walls if you give thanks for what you have. You have a beautiful gift inside. You are love and we are here to support you in knowing this. Tune in deeply there is a place inside you that is whole and has never been wounded. When you are triggered it is a bit harder to find. Be still. Stillness is there and we are here."

The Angels through Dawn Lianna

Chapter Six

Your Angel's Gift & Sweet Heart

Now that you have been practicing, becoming more aware of your inner senses and calling in your Angels daily, we are ready to move forward. Last time we called your Angel and asked for a name. If you have not yet received your Angel's name or names, continue to listen for them. If you have received the name, use it.

Today we are going to continue the same exercise where your Angels come in front of you. This time we are going to do a gift exchange.

The second thing you are going to learn to do is connect to your Angel's heart. Thirdly, you will learn about your body Angel. Take out your journal so you can write down what you are learning.

Angel Gifts

Angels love to share gifts with you. They will even bring you birthday presents. Gifts from the Angels are very real, even though they may be in the inner world. They also can bring you external gifts. Today we are going to journey for an inner gift.

You can also give gifts to your Angels. You can give them anything your imagination can dream up or anything your heart desires. These can be pledges, promises, hopes and dreams, imaginary hearts and flowers, imaginary kittens, seashells, crystals and other offerings. It doesn't matter a hill of beans if they are imagined or physical objects.

Gift Exchange with Your Guardian Angel

1. Ground and center yourself.

2. Know that your Angels are right with you. They are watching your back. Ask them to move around in front of you as you have done before. If you feel vulnerable, ask one Angel to move to the front and another to stand behind you to watch your back. Remember, they can hear you and are moving right now to a new position.

3. Imagine your Guardian Angel in front of you, getting down on one knee, so that your Angel is looking right into your eyes and heart. Feel your Angel's love. Take it in deeply. This is a very real and sweet love. You want to really spend some time experiencing this love.

4. Respond by giving your Angel a gift from your heart. You can give your Angel

anything you can imagine. Whatever your heart feels to give is correct.

5. Now ask your Angel for a gift from your Angel's heart. Be very, very still. Listen, feel and receive. Notice feelings of warmth, impressions and pictures. What did you receive? Right now my Angels handed me a whole armload of long- stemmed red roses. They thanked me for writing about them. How sweet.

6. Stop right here and wait until you know what your gift is. Ask what your gift represents. Imagine placing it in your heart or wherever you feel to keep it. Carry your gift with you.

7. Give big, juicy thanks to your Angel.

Notice that this only took a very few minutes of clock time and notice how good it feels. You can do this anytime you want and you can do it as often as you want. This will help you get a stronger connection to these amazing beings and I know you want that.

A gift exchange is also a way of accepting information. The gift may be the message you have been longing for.

Write down what you have received.

Connect to Your Angel's Heart

We are going to take this exercise another step and connect to your Angel's heart. I am excited to share this with you, as this can be an exceptionally powerful experience. Do this exercise when you have 15 or 20 minutes of quite time available.

Exercise: Connect to Your Angel's Heart

1. Ground and center yourself and put up your tube of light. Fill up with light.

2. Call your Guardian Angel and invite him or her to come around in front of you. After you make a connection, ask your Angel to turn around so that his or her back is to you.

3. When you are ready, lean onto the back of your Angel, placing your heart right over the back of your Angel's heart. Lean right into the delicious sweetness of your Angel and make a very real heart to heart connection. Breathe in and feel your heart filling up with love and opening wide.

4. Melt into your Angel's heart and feel your Angel's magnetic strength. Relax. Trust what you sense and feel. Take all the time you want. You may feel like you never want to lift up from this luscious moment, but

eventually the experience will come to a close.

5. When you and your Angel are complete, allow yourself to sit and relax for a few minutes enjoying the sensations.

This can be an amazing experience. I have done this journey many, many times and taught it to many people. It's one of my all-time favorite practices.

Patty's Angel Gift Story

"Yesterday I did the gift exchange exercise. I gave my Angel a soft velvet, pink heart representing my love and gratitude. She received it very lovingly. I could feel that she cherished it.

In return, I received a diamond on the inner from my Angel. I asked my Angel what the gift meant. She told me, 'Your diamond represents the truth of your life path and your work in the world.' I was surprised and very grateful."

Sonia's Angel Heart Story

"I love, love, love connecting to my Angel's heart. The feeling of his pulsing wings gives me the greatest joy. I find that when I do this in class with a group of people, my experience is sometimes even stronger. If you let go, it's a fantastic experience."

Michelle's Angel Gift Story

"I experienced a visit from a lady Angel. She was very beautiful and her whole being was blue as was the ethereal mist around her. She came and stood right in front of me and she felt comforting and motherly.

She held out her hand with a gift while gazing down upon me.

It was a crystal ball of light with lots of energy that fit in the palms of my hands. She told me I was to use this for healing others as well as myself. She stayed with me for a while and I felt calm and at peace when she departed.

When I meditate now, I hold this ball of light energy in my hands and it brings me healing. I can still vividly picture the angel with clarity and bright color."

A Message from the Angels

"When you lay your heart against our heart, we feel your love. We are deeply honored by your willingness to connect with us and we will find many ways to show you how real we are.

As we sound our trumpets for you, listen with your hearts. Your inner senses will open more and more with time. As you practice your listening skills, include listening with your whole body. It is full of many chakras and subtle sensors. We are so happy to be participating with you.

Stay in your peace. Move with anything that increases your faith and your joy. We are far more able to come through to you when you are in joy and trusting that we are right here. Watch for signs.

We have many gifts for you. They all come from our love. Our love for you is deeper than the deep, blue sea. We love you beyond measure and we hope that everything in your good life is smooth and empowering. We are here wishing all the best for you and cheering you on. We love to talk to you, so ask us any questions about your life. We will find a way to show you our answer."

The Angels through Dawn Lianna

Home Play

1. Call your Angels and exchange gifts with them. You can exchange gifts with them on a regular basis, it's perfectly okay.

2. Receiving gifts is great in and of itself, and it is also a way of receiving information. If I am having difficulty with something and want help, I might ask my Angels for a gift regarding that topic. Remember that a gift can be the message.

3. Open your heart and connect to your Angel's heart daily. Ask your Angel to come around front and turn his or her back to you. Lean your heart onto your Angel's heart. The more frequently you do this, the faster your connection will build, and your heart will open wide.

4. Please document these experiences in your Angel journal.

A Loving Message From the Angels

"The more you pay attention to your feelings, the more joy you will run through your being. When you pay attention you will choose joy and when you choose joy, you feel better. Let the better manifesting begin. Keep a wonderful feeling as we wrap our loving wings around you. As you imagine and feel our love here with you, and you feel love, think of the good things that are coming to you. Be love and manifest from there."

The Angels through Dawn Lianna

Chapter Seven
Your Body Angel or Body Deva

In addition to your Guardian Angel you also have an Angel who is in charge of helping you with your physical body. Your body Angel is sometimes called your body deva. This Angel is in charge of the health and well-being of your physical, mental, emotional and spiritual body.

It is important to be in touch with your body Angel because this Angel helps you with your energy. He or she can be helpful to you with things like eating, working out, finding a health practitioner, correcting a stubbed toe, mending a cranky joint, relieving depression, clearing a foggy head and getting answers to your health questions.

Your body Angel may live next to you somewhere in your aura. Some people feel them over their head or shoulder and others say they live inside their body with them. You can ask for your body Angel's name. Listen and accept what you get, as sometimes it's a surprise.

If you have an open minded or sensitive child, it's good to introduce your child to his or her body Angel. When your child is going through a tough time like an illness or puberty, his or her body Angel can help them with the experience.

Here's an example of how to call your body Angel: *"I call my body Angel. Please come and help me with my body."*

Now we will do an exercise to help you connect to your body Angel.

Exercise: Get to Know Your Body Angel

1. Ground and center yourself.

2. Picture your body Angel in front of you. Imagine your Angel has a very big voice. In other words, know that you can hear her.

3. Ask for specific help. Open your inner senses. When you receive an answer, write it down.

4. Continue to talk to your body Angel. Whether or not you hear your Angel, your Angel hears you. Tell your body Angel the challenges you are having with your body and how you need help. Be specific in your requests.

5. Send your body Angel on a mission to find the help you need. Over the next few hours and days notice the signs, signals and

synchronicity in your life. Those could be your answers.

6. When you are complete, return to your waking consciousness and write down every clue or symbol that came up.

Charlie's Body Angel Story

"I was fishing in the ocean when I met the Angel of my body. I know that I have a Guardian Angel, but this Angel was different. This Angel was so close to me that it felt like it was inside my body or my soul. I had not experienced that in the same way before. I was surprised.

I got a very strong feeling, almost like a memory or déjà vu. The Angel of my body told me to go home and not go any further out to sea that day. I was startled because the seas were calm and I could see nothing coming that looked foreboding. I tried to ignore the feeling but it wouldn't go away.

Then a second thing happened. I got overwhelmingly hungry and I didn't have much food on the boat. The hunger and the message were so strong that it was distracting me. I finally gave in and decided to give up my fishing trip. I went back to shore and ate a meal in a restaurant at the dock.

To my surprise, the sky suddenly grew dark and ominous. Rain started to pour down in torrents. I sat in that restaurant so grateful that I had listened to the voice of my body Angel and my body."

The Overlighting Body Deva Angels

The Overlighting Body Angels are a group of Angels in charge of helping us with our bodies. They are the overseers of those who help with our body. They are different from your personal body Angel in that they are a full team of Angels, of which your personal body Angel is a part.

Call this group in to help you anytime you are dealing with something physical. They are especially helpful in helping you find solutions to physical challenges. Ask them and then let go and see what show up. Here is a little exercise to help you.

Exercise: Overlighting Body Angels

1. Ground and center yourself.
2. Call on and imagine the Over-lighting Body Angels are with you.
3. Imagine a beautiful crystal bowl in front of you and pretend you can place your body issue in the bowl. Ask the Angels to take

care of the situation and bless it. Leave it in the bowl.

4. Go about your day.

5. At the end of the day pay attention to the Over-lighting Body Angels and your bowl again. Check in. How does the situation in the bowl appear? Does it look different? Are you ready to leave it in the bowl or take it back to your body? Allow it to be there as long as you wish to incubate. If you leave it there, check in tonight before you go to bed.

6. Continue to talk to your Angels. Be specific in your requests and pay attention throughout the day and night for clues. You just may stumble upon something new.

A Message from the Body Angels

"We are right here with you as are many Angels. We are here to help you with your physical, emotional, mental and spiritual bodies. As you lie down to sleep at night, stop for a moment and just rest. Call us in. Tell us how your body is doing. Describe for us in detail, the aches, pains, joys and wonders of your body. Tell us what you are grateful for and sad about.

As you tell us your worries and your cares, turn

them over to us. Place your situations in our wings for the night and then pay attention to your dreams. Believe with all your heart, because it is true, that we will help you."

The Angels through Dawn Lianna

Home Play

Spend some time contemplating your body deva. Each day take a few minutes to tune in. Pay special attention to where you feel this Angel in your body. Is he or she inside you, next to you, over you or where? Use the imaginary crystal bowl from the exercise on a frequent basis to allow the Angels to help with your body situations.

A Loving Angel Message

"We are here. Your intention to connect with us increases the possibility of our love coming through. Can you feel our love right now? Pay attention to your inner senses, your feelings, your pictures, the sounds and urgings in your head and in your being. This knowing increases as your intuition flows and as you invite us into your life. As you invite us into your life, so many good things will happen that you did not expect."

The Angels through Dawn Lianna

Chapter Eight
Get to Know the Archangels

Now we are going to meet the amazing Archangels. I love them so much.

Archangels are abundantly present on Earth at this time. We are in the change of an era and that is the time that people need the most help finding their way and staying in equilibrium.

The Archangels are the Angels you have seen most often in pictures with their tall, arched wings. You might have seen them featured in stained glass in churches and cathedrals, engraved in mausoleums, carved into statues, painted on postcards, Christmas cards and other places. People absolutely love pictures of Archangels.

We are lucky to be building a connection to the Archangels. They really are amazing. Archangels attend to humanity in loving and protective ways. They work directly with the ascended masters, your Spirit Guides and ancestors as well.

Each Archangel has specific qualities. Some are here to comfort and nurse us through our wounds; some to support us during transition times; some to guide and counsel us and help us forgive. Others help us with our relationships. Some are here to protect and encourage us. As many human qualities as you can think of, there are Angels to support those areas of our lives.

I don't have the final say on how Angels look, feel or sound. I am just a person like you hoping to continue to make a deeper and deeper connection.

We are each intuiting for their subtle presence. They appear to us in ways that allow us to sense them and feel safe. Each person experiences the Angel's uniquely, sometimes gently and sometimes powerfully. While I might experience an Angel or Archangel as a blazing white light, you might see him or her as a soft subtle blue. Sometimes they appear as the winged beings you have seen depicted in churches, cemeteries and Christmas cards. Many perceive them this way. Other times they appear as balls of light or as sacred geometry of light. However they appear, they radiate divine love.

The Archangels are a unique band of Angels. They have ultra-tall, shoulder-like wings that arch up high and come down long toward the ground. Their wings and their presence are strong and protective. Archangels are such grand beings that I am certain that even those of us who see, sense and hear the Angels, can only fathom a drop of knowledge of these enormous being.

In previous times the male Angels, such as Archangel Michael, have been widely written about. Now the female Angels are also coming forth. They call themselves the Matri-Archangels. These motherly female Angels are stepping forward now to become known and to lend us deeper and greater support.

Their sustenance and care can be nurturing to the deepest parts of your heart. Their own mission is fulfilled when we invite and allow them to help us.

It is said that Angels live 144,000 dimensions deep, yet they visit us here in 3-D. If they are coming that far to serve us, think how much they must love you and all of us. As you call in the Archangels for yourself, call them in for humanity. Ask them to help all of us and to bring peace to our planet as well as your personal world.

Introducing Archangel Metatron

I want to introduce you to the magnificent Archangel Metatron. I often feel he needs a loud drum roll, but Archangel Metatron is as humble as he is loving and huge. Archangel Metatron is the leader and Guardian of the Guardian Angels. He even watches over your own personal Guardian Angel.

He is a great Archangel to call when you need extra help and protection. He is the protector of the protectors and a helper to healers all over the world. If you are in a special situation and need some help, ask Metatron to bless you and your Guardian Angel. You can also ask Metatron to bless a friend and your friend's Guardian Angel.

Archangel Metatron is so immense, it's hard to see and feel his whole being. When you call in Archangel Metatron, legions of Angels come with him, and sometimes they arrive on horseback! Metatron looms above the room, and way above the whole world. When he arrives feel his protection set in. He adores all, and for those of us who are here in service, he adds an extra wing to your back.

Archangel Metatron is omnipotent and available to all. He is helping to bring in and anchor the new light of the world.

Archangel Metatron brings deep strength, grace and a firm peace that can fill you with vitality. He is invincible, and that will radiate to you. Call in Archangel Metatron right now and feel his majestic energy.

A Message from Archangel Metatron

"Dearly beloved ones, we, Archangel Metatron and team are here for you and we love you beyond measure. We are here to support the evolution of humanity. You who are reading these words are very dear to our hearts. You have come far to get to this point. You have traveled light years on your path already and we know you have worked hard.

We congratulate you as you reach this turning point of evolution, where people are looking more deeply to spirit again. We are representatives of Source love. All love comes from our creator, who we serve. As you serve each other in love, you emanate your highest calling."

Archangel Michael

One of the best known of the Archangels is Archangel Michael. People know him all over the world. He protects us and helps us evolve in every way. Michael has extreme confidence, and connecting with him causes one to feel self-assured, courageous, hopeful and to want to move forward in perfect alignment. I feel so guided when I connect with him. He leads us to the center of our path.

Michael stands tall with his sword and shield held high or at his side. He is surrounded by countless Angels ready to serve. Michael has humungous wings and stands so strong. He is so caring of each of us. Call Michael when you're scared, need protection, or want help clearing obstacles, beliefs and issues. Michael and his team are known to help us cut cords, free us from the past and end unhealthy connections to others.

Besides your own Guardians, Archangel Michael is a great being to call when you encounter darkness of any kind: spiritual, psychic, another person or your own shadow. He cuts cords to your past in a flash with his mighty sword. He places his wing between you and potential disaster so fast that you may not have even seen it coming. He can clear a room of bad energy and refill it with light very quickly.

As strange as it may sound, Michael is one of my best friends. He has saved my life more than once, and I love him. Seeing Michael on the inner is like looking at a giant. He will often have to duck to fit in a building, but he can also shrink down into a tiny desk Angel, if you need him to. He doesn't like to scare anyone, as he is all about full support and love. I hope you can see and feel him. His presence is the easiest of the Angels for some people to feel.

Michael is always in alignment with the divine plan and the higher purpose of life. He will stand by your side and support you when you feel called to move forward with a new project or to a whole new life.

Archangel Michael is a protector of every single person and can be in all places at once. Call on him day in and day out to protect you. This can be for a situation that is up in the moment, or something that has been scaring you for a long time. He will help protect and keep you out of harms way. He is also really good at helping us let go when it is time to do so. He will literally stand between you and the thing or person you need to release, protecting and helping you with great compassion.

An Experience with Archangel Michael

I had a very special experience in Europe, in the summer of 2012. I was traveling in Italy with my friend, Elena. We were having a wonderful time. One particular day though we were having a challenging time on the train. We kept running into some rough, hoodlum men. We were nervous, so we asked the Angels to help us and keep us safe.

We were standing in Cinque Terre waiting for our next train, when suddenly I noticed an especially tall, handsome man near us with a beautiful woman on his arm. They were unusual in stature, height and beauty. They were both more than model gorgeous. He was probably 6'3" and she was at least 5'11".

I glanced at my friend and she had already noticed them too. We agreed they seemed Angelic. On the inner, he especially, appeared to have huge Archangel wings.

I heard a man's voice in my head. It said "we will be with you and watch over you, until you get to France on the train. We will make sure you arrive safely." I turned to see if the gentleman was looking at me but he wasn't. I tried hard not to stare because he was unusually gorgeous.

The train arrived to pick us up and we climbed onboard. The brilliant couple sat right behind us, and everyone acted as if things were normal. They didn't acknowledge us, but there was an immense feeling of protection surrounding both of us, as if a bubble of light and safety had come. We both relaxed in the glow of it, as the train went down the track.

At the second train stop, the couple got up to leave the train. They walked through the aisle in front of me and toward the door. My friend's back was to them, as I watched them depart. As they started to leave the train, I internally hollered, "Wait, thank you."

The man turned immediately and put his hands on his heart moving his arms as if to open his heart. He smiled and blew me a kiss. I nearly fell out of my seat! My own heart flew wide open, as it had been touched by a huge beam of love.

My friend saw the look on my face and asked me what had just happened. She said, "Your heart just opened wide." I said, "Yes, the Angel sent me a blessing." We turned to look and the couple was gone. Had it been long enough for them to walk away? I don't know. It could have been but they had disappeared remarkably quickly. I spend days integrating the heart opening experience, the gorgeous Angel blew my way.

Thank you with my whole heart dear Angel, wherever you are. And as I say that right now, I hear "You are so welcome, my love. It's me Archangel Michael, your good friend." I didn't know until this very moment, as I am writing this to you, who the Angel was. When I ask now about his girlfriend, he says that's my lovely Lillianna.

I felt so blessed then and now. The rest of our trip was extra special and the uncomfortable situations stopped.

The Point of the Story

The point of the story is to remember to ask for help. It's a rare and special day that an Angel manifests in physical form and sometimes it happens. The Angels are there for you, whether you see them or not, so please ask for their help. I often ask for it right out loud. They do come and they are here with you right now. As my friend Nancy reminds me, sometimes the hardest times are when we forget to ask for help.

A Message from Archangel Michael

"I am here for you at all times, wherever you are, all over the world. I treasure you. You are a magnificent being of light. I am here to protect you and serve you. Call on me when you are sad, mad, glad, hurt, angry, depressed or scared. I will always be right there. I am in all places at the same time, so know I am with you. I remind you that you are love."

Archangel Gabriel

Archangel Gabriel is a beloved sweetheart. He is known as the great messenger of the Gods. He reminds me of mighty Mercury in the sense that he delivers messages, from a simple nudge to those of the highest caliber and great importance. He carries a trumpet to announce his presence and will sound his horn to get your attention. Beloved Archangel Gabriel has a message for each one of us.

Whenever you have messages in our inner mailbox that you have missed, Archangel Gabriel will try to get your attention. He will deliver your spiritual voice mail.

Call on him and then pay close attention. You might notice a tap on your shoulder, a whisper in your ear, a billboard, newspaper or magazine. You may get more emails. Pay attention to any themes and messages that are showing up. He is there helping you.

He can even help you write in your Angel journal. You might try using automatic writing to bring in his messages. Sit with your notebook and your pen in hand and ask Archangel Gabriel to guide your writing. Let his words flow through your hand. You might hear them first, or you might simply find yourself writing by inspiration.

If you are working too hard and laboring over something, Archangel Gabriel might get you up, encourage you to move around for a while or invite you to rest. How many times have we tried really hard, and then let go, took a nap or shower and found your answer? He will find a way to get your message to you.

I feel close to Archangel Gabriel. He is a supporter of leaders and teachers. He will help you stand in your power and speak your truth.

Gabriel has also been called the Archangel of dreams and clairvoyance. He is deeply connected to our intuition and our destiny, two of my favorite things. Ask him to help you use your intuition to connect with the Angels.

It is said that Archangel Gabriel knows the destiny of each of our souls. He's the go-to guy if you need help finding your life path and purpose. Ask him to help and watch, as he draws your attention to little things and simple tasks. He might nudge you to get up and go to the grocery store where you meet someone who has a message for you. He is here to help keep us on track.

I like to call on Gabriel when I'm writing. He's one of the two Angels who came in my near death experience that I told you about. He seems to nudge me when I've written enough, or when I need to pay attention because there is more information just outside my peripheral awareness. Right now as I am writing, I feel him here. He nudges me to open my healing channels wider so that his Angelic energy can be felt in the writing and the healing energy will flow through the book. He says the better connected I am as I write the more you will be able to feel him in the words. Of course!

One morning, I was writing about Archangel Gabriel. I kept getting the feeling that he was tapping me on the shoulder to pay attention. I had the feeling that some information I have been hunting for was coming to the foreground.

Within minutes, I got a commercial email that had the information hidden inside. If I hadn't been on alert, I might have missed it as it was in a commercial, which I seldom pay attention to. I also noticed that someone had given me a really similar message a few days before, but I had missed it. Thank you, Archangel Gabriel!

A Message from Archangel Gabriel

"You each and all came here with a purpose, a purpose that your soul carved out for you before you came. There are many signposts along your path to mark your destiny or your soul's choices for you.

Pay attention. We will nudge you in the right direction, but it is you who must listen to the urges and the rightness of any action before you take it. When you are clear, follow through and walk the path of your life destiny with confidence, clarity and love."

Archangel Raphael

Archangel Raphael is a great helper for all things emotional. He is there to help us heal and clear our past. He is powerful and he is also very soft, compassionate and loving. To me he has a quiet, tender voice, and can be counted on to show up anytime I need an Angel hug.

He works deeply with the subconscious mind where our past memories are stored. Call on him when you or someone is emotionally upset, doing any emotional clearing work, or life regression therapy. He is a great helper when someone is dying and also helps those who are suffering with loss and grief.

Archangel Raphael Loves Children

I'm sure all Angels love children. Archangel Raphael is especially tender towards children, as they are part of his deepest stewardship. He helps you with your inner child, your birth children, the children you work with, all the children in your life, and even an animal that you regard as your child.

Call Raphael as well as your child's Guardian Angel, if your child is in need. There are so many things that come up for children: friends move, a doll gets lost, schools change, a bully was mean, or they go through puberty and may not feel popular. Raphael can help you with any of these issues.

Archangel Raphael is connected to the healing arts, people who are in need of healing, and those who are offering healing. He loves all forms of medicine, from East to West, traditional to alternative. He loves natural medicine and also respects the science of healing.

Archangel Raphael accepts all paths to healing without judgment of any. When he is helping, you may be guided to any type of approach. Be open and listen for guidance. As you are encouraged, tune in to what feels right for you and follow through.

A Message from Archangel Raphael

"There is a beautiful child inside each of you. You are all loved beyond measure and you are love itself. When you think of yourself as a treasured soul, think of a child who is deeply loved.

You came with a purpose, and you have many feelings that lead you toward that purpose. There is often a lot of clearing that needs to be done to get to your purpose and fulfill your life mission. We are happy to help you."

Archangel Chamuel and Team

The next Archangel team that steps forward to be with us is Archangel Chamuel and team. His name means unconditional love. I've heard the name pronounced too ways, like Samuel with a Ch at the beginning, or Kam-u-el. I use the first.

He is traditionally considered male, yet Archangel Chamuel sometimes comes as male and sometimes female. He/she is androgynous and mutable.

Right now, Archangel Chamuel is actively participating in creating and anchoring the bridge between the divine masculine and the divine feminine, in us and on Earth.

Archangel Chamuel is a leader who helps us make good choices. Take a ride on his back to rise up for the eagle view. Fly above your situation and the Earth to gain perspective. As you lift up to peek in, you can call forth something more positive. He has high hopes for us and for the planet.

Archangel Chamuel and his team are believers in positive, meaningful relationships, and can help you create them.

Archangel Zadkiel and Team

Archangel Zadkiel's team is full of compassion and mercy. They will help you to forgive in even the harshest situations. Call on these Archangels when you need help giving or receiving forgiveness. He works closely with Saint Germaine, the keeper of the violet flame.

Archangel Zadkiel and his team are there to help us transform and purify our lives. When the going is tough, call them in to help you cut lose and regroup. They are good at helping purge the endings and start anew.

In any time period after something has ended, and you are still trying hard to forgive, they are a great team to have around. They have a sense of humor in the letting go process. They will help you learn your lessons and figure out what your soul wants to learn. We are in times of such big change. Let them help you.

There are things that have happened in each of our lives that feel like they have violated us deeply. That is true. We experience this kind of pain and it is hard sometimes to forgive. When relationships come to a close, when a job is ending due to a problem, when you must let go and forgive, call on Archangel Zadkiel's team to help. They help us release the negative thoughts and hurts we have about others and ourselves, with deep, compassionate strength.

Exercise: Get to Know the Archangels

1. Find yourself a comfortable place to sit or lay down for 15 or 20 minutes. Choose a time when you won't be interrupted and take the phone off the hook. Ground and center yourself.

2. Call your Guardian Angel, and then invite in the Archangels. Call Metatron, Michael,

Gabriel and Raphael by name. Invite in any other Angels you wish to have join you.

3. Sense the difference between your Guardian Angels and the Archangels that you have invited. They have a different vibration.

4. Spend a few minutes now and dialogue with the Angels. Remember, they can hear every thought you have and they are responding. Spend as long as you want communing with them.

5. Ask the Angels to wrap their wings around you, and melt into their wings. Feel the immense comfort of their protection and love.

6. Ask them to stay with you throughout the day and night. If you have children or a loved one, that you would like their help with, ask them to stay with your loved ones day and night.

7. When you are complete, ground again. Take notes in your Angel journal.

Your Archangels' Message

"Together we stand stalwart in our stewardship to guide and guard you and your destiny. You each have a special purpose for incarnating. There is no

greater purpose than to be a loving human being.

We remind you, it is no better to be a janitor, musician or a president. What matters are that you love and care for each other. Your destiny is unique to you. We are here to help you stay on the center of your path, and protect to you with our wings of love."

Home Play

1. Continue to ground your energy to Earth daily. Pay special attention this week to the energy of the Archangels. Call them in every day.

2. Notice the difference in energy between the Archangels and your Guardian Angel. Listen, sense, watch and feel for their messages. Pay attention for their signs and signals in answer to your requests.

3. Call each of the Archangels mentioned in the lesson. Call Metatron, Michael, Gabriel and Raphael independently so you get to know them better. Spend some time with each of them. They are all wonderful to know.

4. At least once this week, lie on your Angel's back and tune into his or her heart. Watch to

see if you become a kinder person as a result.

5. Document your experiences in your journal.

A Loving Message From Your Angels

"All desires are wishes for good feelings. When you dream of a special place, you are wishing for the good feeling. Let the good feelings roll.

Be peaceful. Move toward that which gives you peace. Watch for signs from us today. There may be an amazing synchronicity, a gift from heaven. Our love for you is broader and deeper than the ocean. There is no end to our love for you. We want to be in your life. Pay attention. Notice our signals."

The Angels through Dawn Lianna

Chapter Nine
Introducing The Matriarchal Angels

As we shift into new energies on our planet, we find more and more divine feminine energy coming forward. Corporations with women on the board are more successful than those without. Women are respected in positions of power. Men are developing their soft feminine qualities. We are listening even more to our intuition, and people are becoming more sensitive. More people are taking an interest in being in tune with their inner voice. The divine feminine is helping us to birth new energy.

The male energy has been leading the planet for a long time. The same is true on the inner realm of the Angels. Until very recently, whenever I've looked in on the Angels, the male Angels have been the first to arrive. The females were somewhere in the background, where I could barely see them.

When I began writing this book, I started working with the more traditionally known of our beautiful Archangels, Metatron, Michael, Gabriel and Raphael. I knew them better and have worked with them for a longer time myself. They were safe and familiar and I could write about them easily.

When I began to research the feminine Angels, I found less literature on them, so I had to go directly onto the inner realms for the information I needed. I was surprised, pleased, and excited when the Divine feminine Angels showed up and introduced themselves to me as the Matriarch Angels.

When the Matriarch Angels are present you may feel their nurturing presence. They are infinitely wise and loving.

A Matriarch is a.family or social system where a feminine person or being is charge of the leadership. In this case the Matriarch Angels are saying they are taking and have taken the lead.

The Matriarch Angels

Think of the qualities of a perfect mother, who has infinite love for you. This mother loves you no matter what. She loves you when you are laughing yourself silly and when you are crying your heart out. She cherishes you. Her love doesn't wax and wane like a human mother. It is stable and infinitely available. She doesn't care if you've been bad or good. She loves you inside and out.

The female Angels travel in teams. I seldom see them solo. They travel together, often move in bands of color and in patterns of a figure 8.

Matriarch Angel Team Muriel

The first team to step forward wanting me to write about them, so they could meet you, are the Matriarch Angels of compassion who introduced themselves to me as Team Muriel. While Muriel is an individual Angel, she is also present as a team of Angels.

She and her Matriarch Angels are extraordinarily beautiful. They encourage your awareness of the greater plan of all things. They offer us the "higher" view and help us rise up above the troubles of life to a compassionate perspective. Whenever you need perspective, call in Team Muriel. They will remind you of the immensity of your soul.

Team Muriel comes to me today and says, *"Please tell everyone how much we love them and that we have infinite compassion for the struggles of human life. In the inner realms we do not know struggle. Incarnating on Planet Earth is a unique experience. It is designed so that you forget and can recover the knowledge of who you are. While you live in duality, there is a deeper place where you do not. We have complete and total compassion for you in the forgetting of who you are and in the human experience of highs and lows. Call on us to help you through every difficult time you ever have."*

Matriarch Angel Team Haniel

I love Archangel Haniel and her team. Archangel Haniel is attributed with natural healing and strong intuition. As a lover of deep unfathomable intuition, I am very fond or Haniel and her team. They will support you in listening to and trusting your inner voice, even when it goes against all the odds of life. They are so beautifully supportive.

Her team helps to fill you with vitality and passion. She is one of my patron Angels, as a teacher and of intuition, and she helped me for a long time before I was even aware of who she was. She loves your psychic nature, as is the voice of your soul and spirit self. It is how the God/Goddess within you speaks to you. When you want to trust and further develop your intuition, ask for her sweet help.

Archangel Haniel and her team assist us with new beginnings, good luck and a fresh start. Archangel Haniel is often seen as a blue, white opalescent Angel. Traditionally, her name means Grace of God and I think of her as the Grace of the

Goddess. You might see her and her team dancing in moonlight.

Her team brings good luck. Whenever they are near, providence is near by. If you are worried or fearful about anything, ask her team to help you release your burden and find relief.

Call on Archangel Haniel and her team to support you with anything related to healing. Like Archangel Raphael, she works with the new Western science and the healing arts.

Archangel Haniel understands and protects your sensitivity. She knows that being sensitive is not always easy in the land of duality. She is divinely loving and wraps her wings around your sensitive nature. She wants you to stand tall, steadfast and strong and listen to your inner voice no matter what.

Matriarch Angel Team Terasita

Matriarch Angel Terasita is one of my favorite Angels. She has been coming to me for many years. She is a divine mother Angel. She carries a baby in her arms and always reminds me that she cherishes me and all of us as a child of the divine. She is sooooo infinitely loving that when I connect with her, it sometimes brings tears of joy to my eyes, heart and soul.

She works closely with Archangel Raphael as a Guardian and lover of children. Ask her to bless the children in your life. Do you remember the traditional picture of a bridge with the Angels watching over the children who are crossing the bridge. Archangel Terasita and her team and Archangel Raphael, among others, are there. See her team standing by Archangel Raphael, at the bridges, crossroads and transitions of your life , ready to help.

Think of a mother raising a child she adores. This mother wants the very best for her child. She wants this child to listen, to walk protected on the streets of life, to ride his bike with his helmet on and to stay out of harms way. This mother wants her child to listen to the voice of his soul and the warnings and urgings that come from within. That is how Archangel Terasita sees you. She sees you as her divine child whom she loves, protects and nurtures. She is here to help you find your way, by listening to your inner voice. She cherishes you like a mother does her own precious child.

A Message from Matriarch Angel Terasita

"You are a child of light. You are a child of love.

Can you pleeeeaase love yourself all the way, all the time? Love yourself through thick and thin and to the very core of your being. You are cherished and we Angels cherish you and are devoted to you. If we were ever to be so slightly saddened, (which we are not!) it would be to see you so hard on yourself. In other words, can you be infinitely kind to yourself?

Celebrate life. Life is to be enjoyed. The memories that you hold and keep joyfully are created through your fun experiences. You can consciously create wonderful and loving experiences. We want so deeply for you to know how much we love, cherish and adore you."

Archangel Terasita through Dawn Lianna

Matriarch Angel Team Arial

Matriarch Angel Arial is another favorite of mine who I often play with in the inner realms. Archangel Arial and her team are one of the planetary teams of Angels serving us today. Archangel Arial is huge, strong and protective and is an individual Guardian for many. She is doing so much work on the planet and with us.

I want you to recognize her vibration because she can help you with so many things. You can't give her too much work. She assures me it's okay to have the whole world call on her, because she can, indeed, hold us all simultaneously.

Archangel Arial is feminine with a very strong and protective vibration. She is powerfully creative and stands strong with you through thick and thin. When you call in Archangel Arial you may see her strong thick pink or white wings curling around you, holding you in her mighty strength.

Archangel Arial and her team are Guardians of the Earth, lovers of nature and are especially protective of the planetary light workers. She knows that many of you are incarnated Angels. Call her in when you are doing planetary work, creative work or healing activities. Archangel Arial will teach you about the pure strength of the divine feminine.

"You are cherished and loved. There is a creative talent in you miles wide. Like a faucet running strong, when the creative juices are flowing you are allowing your creators love to move through you. Creative juices are healing for you and for the world. Open your circuitry wide and let magnificence flow."

The Angels through Dawn Lianna

Chapter Ten
Get to Know the Special Task Angels

Ooh la la! By now, you are experienced in grounding, calling in your Guardian Angel and the Archangels. Please ground yourself and get out your Angel journal.

We are going to explore some ways Angels can help you, and some other types of Angels to call in when you need assistance.

Angels can help you with any topic or area of your life. They don't sensor their help! I'm really excited to share them with you because they are so useful for the practical matters of the world. Call them daily for general life support and for help with specific situations.

Special Task or Project Angels

The Angels who help with specific projects are called special task Angels. You can call them for any purpose. They are a great help with creative endeavors, music, athletics, cooking, financial, health, relationships, gardening, painting, building, selling, creating a business, writing a book and more.

The Money and Prosperity Angels

The first special task Angels I want to introduce to you are the money Angels. Money Angels are connected to the flow of abundance in your life. They are wonderful to have around whether you are feeling abundant or a lack of abundance.

Here's a way to call them: *"Beloved Guardian Angels, please help me to connect with the money and abundance Angels. I request their help with some specific financial situations."*

Once the money Angels arrive and you feel their subtle presence, explain your situation to them. If you can't sense them, speak anyway. They are there if you have called, and they can hear you.

Tell them the specific situations you need help with. After you make your request, let go. Take your mind off your situation.

Be still and listen. Thank them in advance for taking care of this for you. Pay attention to clues, synchronicity and insights. If someone offers you a gift, receive it with gratitude.

If you are worrying, you put energy into the situation you are worried about. Move down to your heart and let go. It 's great fun to imagine a playground in your heart where you inner child can live happily with all that he or she needs.

Dialogue with your Angels and let them know when you sense them and what you need. Angels love to dialogue.

Your Business Angels

All businesses have Angelic helpers whether we know it or not. If you want their help, call in the business Angels. Ask them to help you. Any prayer or affirmative request will work. *"Beloved Angels, thank you for sending the right people to help my business."*

The Traveling and Traffic Angels

When traveling you can call in a traveling team. They will protect you in traffic and from accidents. These Angels might alert you when your car has a problem or if you have forgotten to change the oil. If you ever have a nagging feeling about your car, it could be your intuition picking something up about your car, or it could be your Angel telling you to pay attention, as your car needs to see the mechanic. Sometimes those voices will get really loud and persistent.

Joyce's Late Night Road Angel Story

"A dear friend lived forty-five minutes from my apartment, in a small town, in the upper Mid-Hudson Valley of New York. We met often at her place to connect with each other.

I usually left her place early so I would get home before dark. However, one night we chatted into the wee hours of the morning and it was 2:15 a.m., when I got ready to head home. My friend suggested I sleep in her daughter's room since she was away at college. The long drive home wasn't appealing at that hour yet I don't sleep well in someone else's bed. I opted to head for home.

While driving home, Route 9 had never seemed so still. It felt eerie to me and some old fears were welling up inside me I felt afraid about being alone on this road late at night. I was uncomfortable and regretting my decision to leave

I approached a deserted stretch of highway, crossed a bridge and suddenly, going at 55 miles an hour, all the lights in my car went out! Everything went dark. There were no streetlights, just a dark highway. I barely could see the side of the road to pull over. A few lights twinkled miles away in a residential area. I sat there stunned.

Panic started to seep in. My mind was racing. What should I do? There were no cell phones back then, so I wondered if it would be safe to walk alone toward town. I tried the lights. They didn't work. I wonder if a minute or two had passed? I was panicking and losing track of time.

Suddenly, there was a tap on my window, and a young man was there. "Where had he come from", I wondered?" I thought, "Never mind, here is help." I rolled the window down. I couldn't see his face. He was wearing a fifties style hat and old clothes. He was thin and looked quite young.

He said, "Your lights are out. Would you release the hood?" I did. In almost a twinkling of an eye after the hood was raised, the lights all came on again. Relief flooded through me. The hood came down with a thud.

The young man passed by my car window. "Can I give you a lift or some money?" I asked. I reached for my purse and turned again to speak with him and he was gone.

It wasn't until I got halfway home, relieved at my good fortune, that it dawned on me, that I had seen no one when I pulled off to the side of the road. There were no cars and no lights. Who would be walking on a dark major highway, miles from houses at 2:30 AM? Besides, the lights had all gone out and in a twinkling they had all come on

As the night went on, I began to think that my friend who had arrived on the road was of another world. I felt he was an Angel.

Several years have passed. I have asked many mechanics what would make all my lights go out while driving? What could a person have done to get them all working instantly? I have never received a reasonable answer.

Story: Angels Turn the Pallet in Mid Air

Have you ever had a feeling that your Angel has helped protect you? I was once driving in heavy L.A. traffic in one of the few days of the year, where it was pouring down rain. I was on the freeway and the traffic was going too fast for visibility. I was uncomfortable and driving in the slow lane. The traffic was pushing me forward and I dared not slow down, without creating a bigger traffic hazard.

I started to pray and call in the Angels. I asked them for help and protection. In front of me in this torrential downpour was a pickup truck full of pallets of wood. The pallets were lying on their sides in the truck, stacked vertically next to each other and they were not tied down. They were bumping around and I was getting really nervous.

I was watching the road with wild eyes, squinting to see through the rain to the road, while watching those pallets bouncing up and down in the back of that truck. I knew I was not in a good situation.

Suddenly on a hairpin turn, one of the pallets flew out of that truck and was heading straight for my windshield and right toward my head. I yelled out loud, *"Angels! No!"* I put my hand up to brace the pallet coming straight at me when suddenly grace descended. The pallet stopped in midair, hovering for a split second right in front of my eyes, turned sideways, and fell to the side of the road without hurting anyone. I was astonished and quivering with a combination of fear and gratitude.

I look back at that moment in my mental review with my inner eye open and I see two white light Angels grab that pallet and turn the pallet and fly it off the road. There is no way without divine help that pallet would have turned and fallen. I remember that experience now as if it were yesterday. My adrenaline is pumping when I tell you the story. I have shivers thinking of it.

I have to say to you again, remember to ask for help. I was spared that day. We have all been spared many times. Do you have a time that an Angel helped you? Can you think of even one time in your life where something extraordinary happened and you didn't really understand how it could have gone that well? You had divine intervention. They are here.

Share your story with others. Telling it to someone with receptive ears will strengthen your own conviction and faith. It will also introduce others to the idea of Angels and hopefully encourage them to seek their help.

I'm lucky to have you reading this. The very fact that you believe in the Angels enough to read this strengthens my faith. So thank you and bless you for your good, good heart.

Parking Angels

You may have heard of the parking Angels who can help you get a front row parking spot. I stay very light when I call them.

"Parking Angels, I am going to arrive at this location in about 10 minutes. Please have a great parking place ready for me. I'm very excited to see what spot you have for me."

Then I get really excited and let the feeling flow. The parking Angels may also warn you when the meter maid is coming your way, and when your meter time is about to expire!

Jo's Parking Angel Story

Joanne wrote: "It is a very well-known fact that wherever I go or whomever I am with, I have parking Angels. My close friends love to ride with me, as most often a parking spot opens up for us. Most importantly, I always tell my Angels 'thank you'."

Mother Angels

These are the Matriarh Angels who carry mothering energy. Call on them when you need your mama. I do call them the Mother Angels. They are so comforting and wise. If someone is going through a separation or grief of some kind ,these Angels are an excellent course of nurturance and relief. Any Angel can help, but these are specialists in loving you, as only a mother can.

Father Angels

Call on the Father Angels when you need the divine masculine and the energy of strength and fortitude. Ask them to give you the strength you need and to help you take right action.

Creator and Clearing Angels

Two other bands of Angels I want to discuss with you are creator and clearing Angels. They often work together. The clearing Angels help you dismantle the past. The creator Angels help you create your new life. So whatever you want to get on with creating, ask them to help you.

Creator Angels

These Angels are here to help you with any creative venture. They are in charge of creative energies. When a baby is born, a new and unique life force enters this world. The creator Angels are like midwives who help birth new energy into this world daily. Call on them when you need insight, new ideas or help with any creative project.

"Creator Angels, please come in and help me with this creative project." I often see them arrive and dance through the atmosphere near me. For this writing project, I asked them to help me create something I am happy with and something you can use for years to come.

Clearing Angels

Clearing Angels are those that come in when something is ready to be completed. These Angels are powerful, loving and very good. Though they have a strong name, they are only of the light. They are great at clearing out your past when it's ready to be done. Sometimes when you are creating something, letting go comes first.

Here are some sample situations where they can help you. Imagine an old house has been condemned and needs a controlled burn, the clearing Angels would be perfect helpers.

If you have an old relationship that has grown stale, ask them to help you clear it out one way or another. Ask them to help you clear any old issues that need to be released.

Never request them to destroy another person or a situation. That is a misuse of energy. They are of the light, so they will not do it anyway. Use their energy to help you dismantle the past and release it into the light, so you and the situation can transform.

Send the clearing Angels ahead when you have to go somewhere that is difficult for you. People have used them in many different circumstances: at the courthouse, hospital, gymnasium, to visit a friend in jail, to release an old habit, to help you energy cleanse your home or to clean out excess stuff.

When something doesn't feel right or energy feels yucky, call on the clearing Angels. If you need them in a hurry say, *"Clearing Angels, please hurry. Come clear us now, right now, please."*

Planetary Angels

Planetary Angels watch over us, the global community, and the Earth herself. If you sometimes wonder why it seems like things are a mess on Earth, it's because the Angels cannot interfere with our free will. They can only do what we allow and ask them to do. We humans are ultimately responsible for our actions and the more we call the Angels in to help the better. These planetary Angels are here for the planet herself as well as us. Their stewardship is the care of the Earth.

Universal Angels

Universal Angels appear to me as huge beings with giant wings. They have a nurturing, motherly quality and are also very protective. They are deeply connected to the whole Universe, as well as to Earth and to ourselves. Their stewardship is to help Earth be in alignment to the Universe and to Universal will. When you see them, they stand guard over the Earth.

Cherubs

Cherubs appear as little bubbly Angels. They often appear to humans as children with wings. Remember the old-fashioned Christmas cards with the picture of a child's head with wings? That is the form in which Cherubs often introduce themselves.

Cherubs bring in great joy and are wonderful for lightening up the mood in a room. I love to invite them in and watch them interact at parties and fun events. They love music, song and dance.

The Mighty Alohem

I've had some amazing experiences with the Alohem Angels. The Alohem are harder for me to personally see. They come so some as balls of light. One friend describes them as blue light. I perceive the Alohem as extra tall pillars of light.

The name Alohem means God. They are often called the architects of creation. Some consider the Alohem as creator Gods.

I had the great good fortune of training with a wonderful teacher, June D'Estelle. If ever there was an Alohem in form, it is June. She is a teacher of intuition development and has been since I began walking and talking on this good Earth. She is a way shower and opener of many metaphysical doors.

I sat in meditation with June, for many years, until she retired. Now her students still meet to take turns calling in the Alohem and leading the meditations, as she do kindly taught us to do. The energy of the Alohem is magnificent, strong and pure.

The Alohem are excellent at lifting us up and giving us the higher perspective on any situation. They have a magnificent ability to help you to get the overview of any situation.

Angels Who Walk Among Us

Many of us have a close friend that we are certain is at least part Angel, travels with Angels or acts as an Angel in our lives.

Sometimes people have an experience of someone showing up suddenly and disappearing just as fast at a time when extra protection, care or help was needed. I've shared some of these stories already. Some of us have witnessed an incarnated Angel.

Take a few moments to contemplate the people in your own life, your friends and family. Do some of them have Angelic qualities? Do you have a special friend who calls you for coffee just when you most need a friend? Or a family member who has been by your side too many times to count.

You may have acted as an Angel to another more than once yourself. Contemplate compassionately the people in your life. Some of them may be suffering mildly or deeply. Can you serve as an Angel in their life?

It's of course important to be a compassionate, loving and attuned person. The more you tune in the easier it is to remember your own Angelic nature.

Exercise: Special Task Angels

1. Find a comfortable place to sit or lie down. Choose a time when you will have 20 minutes of uninterrupted time. Turn off your phone, ground and center yourself.

2. Choose a project where you want help from the Angels.

3. Call in the special task Angels that seem connected to your project. Think of the kind of project you are creating and ask for the Angels who are good at that kind of activity.

4. Make a simple prayer: *"Special task Angels, please come to help me with my project. Guides*

and Guardians, help bring the best Angels to help me with this situation. Clearing Angels, come and help me release all that stands in my way."

5. Spend a few minutes listening and tuning in for guidance. Notice your urges. Relax deeply. Pay attention to your senses throughout the day, as the Angels will continue to nudge and support you. Sometimes people feel a wing on their shoulder or cheek. Follow through on your urges. Make notes in your Angel journal.

A Traveler's Angel Story

"One day, I asked my Angels for advice on which park would be best to visit that day. I wanted to try a park across the river in Vancouver that I had never visited. My Angels kept saying, 'No. Go to a park close to home.'

The weather was beautiful and I was in the mood to visit a new park instead of one I'd already been to before. I couldn't think of any reason in my mind why I shouldn't try out the new park. I decided to ignore my Angels' advice and head to the new park anyway.

After 10 minutes on the freeway we ran into a huge traffic jam due to road construction. I didn't know of a good alternative route to head in the direction we wanted to go. It took 30 minutes to get off the freeway and turn around.

Of course, I realized my Angels had been right about staying closer to home. I missed my cues when I ignored them. It would have saved a lot of time and frustration on the freeway if I had listened to my Angels and trusted their advice. Remember to listen and forgive yourself when you don't."

Forgiveness is such an important key to living a good life. Most of us know this and have a hard time sometimes forgiving ourselves. You and your good heart, deserve forgiveness as much as anyone. May the Angels send you an immense volume of self-love and forgiveness.

An Angel Message

"We love you. We are here for your projects. Please be specific in your requests. If you need us to bend and stretch time for you, we can and will. If you need help getting your creative juices going we will help you. If something is getting in your way, we will clear it out. Do you know why? Because we love you.

Home Play

1. Choose a project that you want help with.
2. Ask the special task Angels to help you with your project. Call them in each day this week and make notes in your journal.
3. Continue to ground. Connect with your Guardian Angels and the Archangels. Continue to practice the exercise where you lean onto your Angel's back and melt into your Angel's heart.
4. Document your experiences in your journal.

A Loving Angel Message

"Consciousness expands and yet consciousness is infinite. Think of consciousness as the ocean and your personal consciousness as a drop of water in the ocean. Think of consciousness as a computer full of programs and everyone has access to the same computer. The computer will output whatever data you need but the computer will only output the data that you allow based on the programs you are running. Change the program and you get a different output. The more often you think of us, the easier it is for us to connect to you. We remind you that we see you as pure love."

The Angels through Dawn Lianna

Chapter Eleven
Angels of Hearth and Home

I hope you are enjoying working with special task Angels and are becoming more conscious of their presence in your life. They are surely there to help you.

Before you proceed, ground and center yourself. Get out your Angel journal. Ask your Guardian Angels to be with you, inspire you and help you to learn.

Today we are going to get in touch with the Angel of your home, and learn how to build an Angel altar or sacred space. These ideas are suggestions to get you started. Use your own creativity and intuition to create for yourself a great place to connect with your Angels.

The Angels of Your Own Home

Getting in touch with the Angels of your home is a rewarding meditation and experience. These Angels oversee where you live and are protective of your home, land, community and geopathic zone. Your home (or house) Angels are always present. Your home need not be lavish. Angels don't really care about possessions. Your inner happiness is more important to them. So no matter where you live, know that there are grand beings watching over your abode.

Your home Angels can help you whether you are traveling, whether you own or rent, are on the move, are camping in a tent or even stuck on the street.

I have seen Angels inside of homes and buildings, often at the ceiling level. I have also seen them while driving somewhere hovering over a whole house. It looks to me like the Angel has his wings draped right over the roof. The wings reach all the way to the ground, and often the Angel's head is resting on the rooftop. They sometimes look asleep, though I am sure they are relaxed, yet alert. It's an amazing sight!

What comes to my awareness, when I see these Angels, is how much they love the particular person and the home. The love they are projecting into and around that home is palatable. The effervescence of sweetness on the Angel's face is obvious.

Exercise: Meet the Angels of Your Home

1. Ground and center yourself.
2. Invite your Guardian Angels to come and be with you.

3. Consciously acknowledge the Angels of your home: *"Dear Angels of my home, I would love to get to know you. Please make your presence known to me."*

4. Sit quietly. Contemplate the way you feel in your house. Do you feel protected here? Have you ever seen the Angel or Angels of your home? Can you sense them?

5. Think of some times when good things happened and there was a lot of synchronicity. That may have been your Angel helping you.

6. Whether you are consciously aware of the Angels or not, spend some time talking with them. Ask questions and listen for answers.

7. Tell the Angels about the kind of changes you would like to see and feel in your home, and ask for help.

8. Know that your Angels hear you and work with you purposefully.

9. When you feel complete with the meditation, return to waking consciousness and write in your Angel journal.

Sacred Spaces and Altars

Your home is a sacred space. It is your retreat from the world. It's great to create a sacred place or altar where you can sit to connect with your Angels. Having a special time and place to sit down and relax increases your receptivity, as ritual is a powerful tool. You can use this special place to connect with yourself and any Angels you want to connect with, including the Angel of your home.

Here are some ideas to inspire you to create an altar or a sacred space that is balanced, so that when you sit in that place you are centered.

Use the Elements to Build an Altar

To build an altar using the elements, Earth, air, fire and water, choose an item that represents each of those elements and place them on your altar or in your sacred space.

Element

To include the Earth element, add a gorgeous cloth or a favorite sarong to a table. You might also include a stone, crystal, plant or other natural object. Each of these items represents the element of Earth. Ask the Angels in charge of the Earth element to join you.

Air Element

To include the air element add a fan, a whirligig, windmill, picture of the wind, and a piece of fruit or a flower. Pieces of fruit or a flower represent air as they grow up off the ground. Ask the Angels of the air element to come and bless your altar.

Fire Element

This one is easy, as a candle represents the fire element. You could also light a stick of incense, add a lamp or nightlight, or a beautiful picture of a bonfire or the Sun. Call in the fire Angels now to include them in your process.

Water Element

There are many ways to add the water element. Place some water in an elegant bowl, add a fountain, and include a picture of a lovely lake, waterfall, river or ocean. Even some seashells will bring out the water element. Ask the Angels of the water to come and join you.

When you have each of the elements represented, you have created a balanced space.

Yin/Yang

Another easy way to create a balanced space is to use a balance of opposites. Yin represents the female side and yang represents the male side. The female side is receptive and the male side of life is active. When you use both yin and yang, you create a balanced place.

You can find many yin and yang symbols in your cupboard, at the Goodwill and even in the grocery store. Making this altar can be very easy and inexpensive.

Some examples of yin and yang are opposite colors on the color wheel, a dark and a light stone, the Sun and the moon, a man and a woman, night and day, a desert and the ocean, a picture of two people or two matching Angel figures. Use your imagination and think of pairs that you love. Then place them in a way that feels good to you.

Use the Feng Shui Bagua

For a slightly more complex altar you can build one using the Chinese Bagua from Feng Shui. The areas to represent on your altar are career, wisdom, your ancestors, health, money, fame, relationships, creativity, travel and benefactors. In this scenario, you would include on your altar something to represent each area of your life. Then call in your Angels and ask them to bless all of these areas.

You might consider taking my online course, *Create Wealth with Feng Shui*, at dailyom.com. This course will teach you plenty about traditional Feng Shui, the use of the Bagua and other tools to help you. It's low cost and lots of fun.

Invite in the Masters

The spiritual masters depicted in all the world traditions speak to many of us. You can place pictures of the masters and the Angels on your altar. One of my Spirit Guides is Lao Tzu, so I love to have a statue of Lao Tzu on my altar. Be creative. Add things that bring you joy. Personalize your altar so that when you meditate there, you feel exceptionally good. The idea is to uplift yourself and ask the masters to bless you.

Keep it Simple

My favorite is the simplicity of a candle and a small bowl of water. Sometimes I put a stone in the water. I also love to make sweet little offerings to the Angels as I invite them in. It may be my fantasy that they like candy or other little treats, but it makes me feel good to know I've left something out for them. It's like the old days when I used to leave cookies out for Santa. I know now that my dad ate them, but every once in a while one of my altar cookies disappears too, even when I know I didn't eat it. It makes me giggle to think about that and wonder what happened.

Write a Love Letter to the Angels

Write a letter to the Angels. Write it from the depth of your soul and the bottom of your heart. Make it one of the most sincere letters you have ever written. Tell the Angels all the things you are genuinely grateful for in your life. After you have expressed your gratitude in all respects, express your current wishes and yearnings.

Pour your heart out, knowing they hear you and will support you. Then give your fervent thanks.

Place the letter on the altar. Ask yourself how many days you should leave it there. When this feels complete, it's great to burn the letter with love. As your letter goes up in smoke, see that smoke as taking your prayers to the creator for their realization.

Jaxine's House Angel Story

"I was trying to sell my condo and having a really hard time finding a buyer. I wanted to move, but it

felt like the house was pulling on me to stay. I had conflicted feelings that I didn't really understand.
I decided to talk to the Angel of my home. She told me that her name was Flower. Flower told me that she didn't want me to move because she would miss me. I told Flower that she could move with me and that I'd like her help finding a buyer.

The very next morning, I got an offer on my house. It gave me the chills. The offer went through, and those people did purchase my home. Flower led me to a beautiful new home near the river."

Jan's Altar Story

"I love to make altars in my house. Sometimes I have two or three, or even one in each room. It makes me feel good to see my special things on my altar. Because these spaces are pretty, many of my friends don't even realize that my mantle and my end table are altars to me. They have simple décor and a candle that I light and use when I call in the Angels. To the rest of the world, it just looks beautiful."

A Message from the Angels about Altars

"When you create a sacred space for us, such as an altar or a meditation nook, it helps you to feel our

presence. It creates a vibration and expectation that we will meet up. It also creates a quiet space to do that in.

We are everywhere. Your expectation that we will be there at your altar or anytime you call us is what helps you to connect. Expect to see us right now and here we are!

We are with you at all times. It is not necessary for us to have an altar to be with you. The altar creates a connecting link between us. When you sit at your altar you will receive the energies we have infused into the objects for you. They are full of our love. Enjoy!"

Home Play

1. Call in and get to know the Angel of your home. Spend time communicating with him or her. Tell your Angel what you most appreciate about your home, and give thanks. Then tell your Angel the things you would like to change, and ask for help. Be sure to listen and pay attention with all your senses to receive your Angel's guidance.

2. Build an altar or create a sacred space or mediation area for yourself and your

Angels. Use your creativity and your favorite objects, colors, sounds and smells. Make it as simple or as elaborate as you wish. Experiment with making it feel Zen and balanced.

3. Document your experiences in your Angel journal.

A Loving Message from the Angels

"We carry a shield to protect you. Know that we are here. Call us in daily. With shield held high around you, we protect your precious self. Ask for our help. There is no need to do this alone. We carry a sword to cut the cords of the past from you. Know that we are here. Ask for our help."

The Angels through Dawn Lianna

Chapter Twelve
Get to Know Other People's Angels

I hope you have created a really special altar space for connecting with your Angels. Please continue to connect daily with each of the Angels you are getting to know.

Please ground and center yourself as you start this chapter. Call your Angels to be with you and get out your Angel journal.

Working with Other People's Angels

We are going to learn about working with other people's Angels. It is appropriate to ask your Angels to help you connect with the Angels of a friend, as long as you have your friend's best interest at heart. If you are ever mad at somebody and you ask for something negative to happen to that person, the Angels will not help you. That would not be an Angel's stewardship or wish. They never harm anyone.

We live in free will. As I have said, the Angels will not intervene where they are not invited, so remember to request their help, for yourself or for another. Then they are able to step in and help you. By asking, you open the door and give them greater permission.

You can communicate your love to anyone through your Angels. Inviting the Angels into the middle of any situation can soften the communication. In each of our lives, there are times when we have had a challenge with a friend or when a friend is challenged with a difficult situation. At times like that, it is great to ask your Angels and your friend's Angels to help.

Get to Know Other People's Angels

When you need help with another person, you can ask your own Guardian Angels to talk to the other person's Angels, or you may speak to the other person's Angels directly. Even if you don't hear them, know they hear you.

Here is how to do that. Ask your Guardian Angel to mediate between you and the other person. Send your Guardian Angel and ask him or her to talk to the Guardian Angel of the other person. The Angels will deliver your message with love. The Angels act as a mediator between the two of you.

This cleans up communication quickly and remarkably. The message is transferred to light, and delivered to the person in a way that is easy to hear.

Another strategy is to speak directly with the other person's Angels yourself. You simply ask permission on the inner realms to make a connection to the other person's Angel. Then you tell the Angel the message you want to deliver to the other person. That will work very well for you.

You might want to use one of these strategies when a friend is traveling or has not been communicating with you. You could speak to the Angels of an elderly parent to find out how the soul is doing. You can communicate with the Spirit Guides of your health practitioners, your boss, your employees, your child's teacher, a courtroom judge or with anyone you need support communicating with.

Here are three stories about times that another person's Angels have come to visit their friends.

Kristen's Fascinating Angel Story

"One night in spring I was falling asleep and I felt a warm, loving presence at the end of my bed. I felt that it was the Angel of a good friend. I questioned the Angel and asked why she was there and if my friend was okay. The Angel told me that my friend was fine and that she, the Angel, was sent to join my Angelic team. She would now be working with both of us. I went to sleep knowing that she was with me. The next morning I could still feel her presence.

I emailed my friend and told him about my experience. He wrote back and told me that the night before he had prayed for our Angels to connect. It's awesome to know that my friend and I both love and share an Angel."

Ann's Angel Story

"I really wanted to hear my Angels and as yet I wasn't having a lot of success. Then an old friend of mine came back into my life. I fell in love with him, and then he disappeared again, without communicating the reason for his disappearance. I was sad and upset.

I called on his Angels to help me. Surprisingly, over the next few weeks, his Angels came to visit me daily. I was astonished that I was able to hear them. They helped me cope with the loss of my friend. That experience opened the door to hearing my own Angels."

How to Talk to Children about Angels

Children, of course, have Guardian Angels. I don't know if you were told as a child that you have a Guardian Angel, but this is a very comforting thing for a child to hear. Children often sense subtle energies and may be able to see their Angel.

Tell your child that he has an Angel that protects him. This Angel is with him all the time and loves him as much as you do. Tell your child that he can call on his Angel whenever he is scared, whether you are nearby or far away.

You can also speak to your child's Guardian Angel and ask for help anytime. While still performing your role as a parent, turning over some of the Guardianship of raising and protecting your children to their Guardian Angel can be a relief.

Here are a couple of stories about children and their Angels.

Annie's Miraculous Guardian Angel

"A client called me because his 8-year-old daughter Annie could not sleep at night. She was afraid of something coming to get her in the night. I went to their home to see her. When I spoke with her she told me she was afraid of a dark spirit. I asked her if she was aware she had a Guardian Angel. She said, yes, she had heard of that.

I took her on a guided meditation where she met her Guardian Angel. After that meditation she felt very comforted and told me all about her experience. Children pick this up very quickly. Over the next few days, the results were miraculous. She was able to sleep at night and connect to her Angel.

The next time I saw Annie, she was calm and matter of fact about her contact with her Angel, and told me how her Angel protects her in the night. I could not have been more proud of her."

Emily's Childhood Angel Story

"When I was a little girl, I would awaken at night and make myself upset on purpose, because when I was upset I could feel a warm glow surround me. I knew the Angels would come if I were upset. So I used that as my call to the Angels. Honestly, it was the only way I knew. I could feel a presence at the end of the bed that would slowly come all around me. I saw them as gold and sparkling light. It was obvious to me as a child that these were Angels who had come to comfort me.

In true dramatic style, I would then tell them that I was all right and all this attention was unnecessary. When I was cozy and happy, I would drift to sleep. Now, as an adult, when I am legitimately upset, I can still feel this warmth around me. I know now that I can also call them when I am feeling good."

Exercise: Know Someone Else's Angels

1. Ground, center and clear your energy.
2. Choose a friend whose Angels you would like to connect with. Ask your friend for her permission on the inner or the outer to talk to her Angels. Tune into your own Angels and ask them to be with you.
3. Think about your friend and ask your Angels to help you connect to your friend's Angels. Ask those Angels to make themselves known to you. Ask for any messages that are for you.
4. Stay and commune with them as long as you wish. When you are complete, thank them and return to waking consciousness.
5. Write down your experiences.

A Message from the Angels

"We love to help you with your friends. When you need some extra help with a colleague, employee, friend or family member, call on us. We are very effective mediators. We can smooth and soothe the airwaves between you and soften the vibes so healing and love are restored. We love to help you make more loving connections with others, and you can freely use us for this purpose anytime.

Take care of each other. You too are an Angel. Every time you do an act of kindness for yourself or others, we are made happier."

Home Play

1. Think of a friend whose Angels you would like to connect with. Ask your Angels to help you connect. Send thoughts for your friend's highest good. Ask your Angels to talk with the Angels of your friend. Practice this strategy with at least two people this week. Document your experiences in your journal.

2. Continue to connect with your Guardian Angel and the Angels daily. Continue to use the special task Angels with your projects. Lean onto your Angel's back and feel your heart next to your Angel's heart.

3. Document your experiences in your Angel journal.

A Loving Angel Message

"We offer you our love and comfort. We stand tall and wrap you in our wings of love. We know that sometimes you are not aware of our presence. Open. Open. Open now. We are here. We are with you. Your call is answered before you ask us.

When you ask, we are allowed to step through the door of your heart and into your deeper being to help you. When you call us, you open the door to receive our help. We step in with you, closer and closer to your dimension."

The Angels through Dawn Lianna

Chapter Thirteen
The Healing and Comfort Angels

This is our last chapter and I hope you are enjoying the Angels. Here you will learn about special healing Angels and review the book. I want you to be able to take this work with you and use it for the rest of your life.

As we begin this chapter, please ground and center yourself, call your Angels and get out your Angel journal.

Working with the Sweet Healing Angels

Healing Angels are here to help us in times of crisis and healing. They come in droves when people call them to help. Some of them are big universal Angels, and some seem to shrink down to the size of a pea, to join you quietly in the cells of your body. If you ask them to help you heal, they will do that in the direction of your intention, and within your soul contract.

When you call them, you may notice that things get easier. They might bring healing to you or your loved one. They might also open a door to a better health practitioner, doctor or nutritional resource. Pay close attention to whatever comes your way after you have called them.

Angels of Comfort and Change

Anytime you are feeling lost, scared, ill, or in emotional distress, you can call the healing and comfort Angels. These beings are very warm and loving and are designed to help in time of grief and loss. Ask for their sweet comfort and love to become known to you and let them hold you.

Sometimes you or a friend could be having a hard time changing or learning a needed lesson, and keep making the same mistake over and over again. The Angels of comfort and change can help people learn their lessons.

These Angels are compassion itself. They understand that sometimes we feel stuck and can't move forward, no matter how hard we try. They know there is a wound in the way. Sometimes we are conscious of our wound, and other times the wound is in our unconscious mind. These Angels will comfort your soul, so you can see through the situation to the truth.

They also are fully aware that you are not your wounds. While that may be a stretch for some of you to believe, others know this is true. These Angels will remind your soul again and again who you really are, and you are love.

Grief and Loss

It's time for us to touch in on the special times of deep transition, grief, loss and death. Many people have reported being in touch with Angels in their times of deepest need. When you have a difficult life transition, a loss, your children moving from the nest, a disappointment at work or someone you love has passed over, the Angels can show up to comfort you.

Loss can sometimes be a challenging emotion for a person to process. Several times, in my work as an intuitive reader, I've seen a client has unknowingly experienced a Guide change. Each of these clients were feeling quite sad for no known reason. Upon looking in on the source of the sadness, the Guide team has told me, that one of the client's Guides or Angels has moved on to another position. A person can experience this as a deep loss with no apparent cause.

Be clear that a new Guide has either taken the old Guide's place or will soon step in. We are not left without guidance. We have many Spirit Guides. A Guide may sometimes change, when we are ready for a big change in our life. The new Spirit Guide will be a better fit for our new life. When the person finds this out consciously, there is usually a big sigh of relief.

Loss affects animals similarly and they too, will lie down in a puddle, when someone has moved or died. I've seen a mama dog whose puppies died; hide out in her doghouse for weeks, and another lose her fine temperament when her puppies were sent to a new home. I've seen animals make difficult transitions to new homes and I've seen the Angels there to comfort them.

Angels and Coping with Death

I have seen so many Angels around family and friends at the time of passage of a loved one. They also minister to the person who is dying. They come to escort the soul who in transitioning, to help them cross over into the light, as well as comfort the living family.

I've been asked several times to assist someone who is dying. I once sat with a dying friend at his request and hypnotically guided him over and back across the veil, a week prior to his passing. He wanted to see the "happy hunting ground" as he called it.

When he came back from his guided journey he told me he would die the next Tuesday, and he had no more fear of death. He died peacefully in his lover's arms, the following week, on Tuesday.

I have been called by relatives to help escort a dying loved one across the veil. This is of special benefit when someone is scared to die and it does assure a safe passage to the other side. It's an amazing and blessed experience to escort someone over, and the Angels are always there to help.

The Keepers of Life and Death

The souls passing over are often greeted by a large team of Angels. There is a band of Angels whose main purpose is to help souls cross over. To me they look silver. I call them the Angels with the silver lining.

When Angels come to greet the passing soul at the bridge they will often greet the soul with gifts. The soul is then taken across the bridge where they are often reunited with friends, loved ones and mentors who have passed before them.

My own mother passed over many years ago. I traveled with her halfway across the bridge. There we were greeted by a group of Angels carrying long-stemmed, huge, bountiful red roses. The Angels filled my mother's arms with the roses and then turned to me. They filled my arms with roses also, and said it was time to tell my mom goodbye.

As we made our final hug for this lifetime, a golden white light enveloped us. The Angels told me not to go any further over the bridge, as it could be damaging to my physical body. I bade my mother farewell.

Years later when I had my own near death experience, I saw the same group of Angels again. They highly recommended that when I do this work, I not look too closely at them as their job is to take souls over and it's not my time to go. After these amazing experiences, I have no fear of my own passing.

Exercise: Healing and Comfort Angels

1. Ground, center and clear yourself.
2. Choose a topic around which you have strong feelings that you would like to shift.
3. Allow yourself to tune into these feelings, focus and ask your Angels to help you. Breathe right into your feelings, as this will help them dissolve.
4. Call out to the band of healing and comfort Angels. Ask your Guardians to help you connect to them. They will do this immediately.

5. Ask for these loving beings to wrap their wings around you. Ask them to smudge away your tears and fears and help you feel better.

6. As you continue to breathe, deepen your relaxation. Allow yourself to melt into the comfort of the Angels. Let your muscles relax and your face soften. Ask them to bring comfort to everyone involved in your situation and see them doing that now. Know that it is real and true.

7. Spend as much time here as you wish. When you are complete, thank the Angels. Return to waking consciousness feeling lucky and grateful.

Ron's Story of His Mother's Passing

"My mother, Angeline, left her body in 2003. After the mortuary took her body away, I laid down. In a waking dream, I saw my mother come into the room, race past me and start fixing the bed. Right behind her was her Guardian Angel.

I spoke to her Guardian Angel. I said 'Angie passed a few hours ago. What is next for her?' Her Angel spoke to me. She said, 'Angie is still a little attached to her husband, but she will be moving on shortly.' Then my mother flew out of the room into a corridor of light. I saw her disappear up a spiral of light. I was relieved and comforted.

Her Guardian Angel's face was strangely familiar. A year and a half earlier, I had seen this Guardian Angel's face in a picture. I hunted and found that picture in my mother's drawer. I asked my family members if anyone recognized the person in the picture.

They all said she seemed familiar, but no one knew who she was. I am not sure what this meant, but it was a very touching experience for me."

Alice's Empowering Angel Story

"Many years ago, I received information that was very upsetting and unexpected. As I was trying to absorb it, I suddenly felt a pair of hands holding mine.

I knew somehow that it was my Angel's hands. I could feel her strength supporting me and helping me through this difficult experience. I was and still am grateful."

Carol's Touching Angel Story

"When my daughter was having some problems I sat in my chair to meditate. I saw a picture of her in quicksand trying to get out. I prayed that I be given the strength to help her.

At that point, I opened my eyes and saw a beautiful figure of a woman with dark shoulder length hair in a white gown, trimmed in gold. The loving figure came closer to me and it actually felt like she came into my body.

I somehow knew I would be able to cope with whatever was ahead and the Angel would be with me. The Angel or Guide had no wings. It was a spiritual female being and I had a strong feeling it was an Angel."

Kate's Intense Angel Story

In the following story, notice how Kate describes her experience in deep feelings, pictures and sounds. She also trusts herself deeply.

"The weather was hot and my sleep was difficult. I was awakened abruptly by a phone call. My daughter told me that my grandson was in intensive care. I threw on the clothes nearest me and raced to the hospital.

When I arrived at ICU, I found my beloved 10-year- old grandson, Cody, going in and out of a diabetic coma. With blood sugar levels of 700, all of his internal organs were working to keep him alive.

My first reaction was to break down in tears. I took a moment before entering his room. During my prayers for strength, a white light appeared on the wall across from me. I was fascinated by this light and at the same time I heard a voice saying, 'You can be strong for the family. It is the gift that you can give to them.' The voice sounded Angelic.

I went into Cody's room where I found him unconscious, with nurses surrounding him doing what they needed to do to keep him alive. His mom, my daughter, fell apart in my arms. I knew my job was to assist the people who were helping my grandson.

I held Cody's hand while telling him to be strong. I guided my daughter to take a position opposite me at his side. She also held his hand and spoke of her love for him.

Family members came and went for the first 24 hours while we waited. With each new visitor I would hear the bright light voice repeat the words to me, "You can be strong for the family. It is the gift that you can give to them.'

As the hours advanced I heard the voice say to me, 'Call others to help you in this task. They will be strong for you.'

I obeyed the voice. I made twenty-five phone calls. Each person heard my need and said they would help. We created a prayer chain and turned our distress over to a higher source.

Within a few days, Cody was out of danger. His first words were, 'What was the bright light that kept shining on me while I was so sick?' As reports came back many people who were praying for him remarked that they had seen a bright white light during their prayers. Could this be the same bright light? Was this bright light an Angel? Were we all seeing the same Angel? I think so."

A Heartfelt Message from the Angels

"We are here with you all the time and never so intensely as in your hour of deepest need. When you grieve, we grieve with you. We feel your feelings with you. Our love for you and for your loved ones is incomprehensible in human form, as it is infinite. The supply of love, support and comfort we bring you can never end, because there is no end to love."

Meet Your Angel's Review

I want to send you sailing out with the Angels. While reading this book you have learned how to connect with your Guardian Angel, get a name, receive a gift and hook up with her heart.

You have learned about the Archangels, spent time with individual Archangels and the special task Angels. You learned about your body Angel and the Angel of your home. You learned how to build an Angel altar. We have covered how to work with the Angels of another person and the Angels of healing, grief and loss. If you have been vigilant in doing your homework, you may have experienced a deepened contact with your Angels.

An Enchanting Message from the Angels

"We are right here among you. Those with eyes to see, ears to hear, and senses to feel, will know of our presence. We are here. Remember we are right here with you. Invite us into your mind and heart. Ask for our help and it is given. We love you. We bless you. We appreciate you. We know you are having a human experience, and we know that you are truly a divine beam of love."

Home Play

1. If you have sadness or a loss in your life, spend some time calling in the healing and comfort Angels to help you with your feelings. Breathe into your feelings and watch them dissolve. Ask the Angels to come and wrap their loving wings around you and let go.

2. Notice the expansions that you have experienced since reading this book. Go through your Angel notebook and read your experiences. Look at your original goals and notice your progress. Give yourself a big pat on the back.

3. Continue to call your Angels into your daily life - forever! Practice, practice, practice.

4. Document your experiences in your journal.

Chapter Fourteen
A Joyful Conclusion

I hope by now, you are clear that you are love and that your angels love you beyond measure. They cherish you. They long to be of service. When you invite them in, you increase their opportunity to serve and to connect with us here on earth.

As I have written this book, the angels have visited me many times to bring their messages of love. I am blessed and I feel cherished. My own ability to live in the state of love has increased immensely and my sense of inner peace has become reliable.

I thank you for calling this work forth. I thank the many people who asked me to put this work into form. I love and cherish the opportunity to be of service to you and to the angels. May your entire life be blessed and may there always be 10,000 angels by your side.

Love to you each and all,

Dawn Lianna, M.A.

A Blessing from Your Angels

"You know by now that we touch you in all walks of life. We know that it is sometimes difficult for you to hear us. Be still, tune in and feel. We send soft impressions your way. By calling us, you increase our opportunity to be with you. Call daily: 'Angels! Beloved Angels! Come be with me now!' We are here. Your call is answered before it is made. By calling, you open the door of your own awareness so you may perceive our love and support.

You are cherished. You are a precious child of the Universe. You are cherished just because. You are cherished without lifting your little finger. You are cherished. You are cherished. You are cherished. Remember this now and throughout your day."

The Angels through Dawn Lianna

About The Author

Dawn Lianna, M.A. is the best selling author of six Online courses. She offers intuitive readings and Intuition Development trainings worldwide. Her style is perceptive and truthful, yet gentle, loving and clear. Her favorite, private sessions are those where she introduces you to your own Spirit Guides and Angels.

Dawn was born intuitive and her skills were deeply enhanced by three near death experiences. Those experiences were extremely challenging for her and overcoming them has strengthened her intention and ability to stay in tune with spirit.

Dawn is a lover of life, and enjoys gardening, traveling and hiking. One of her favorite activities is to play keyboard in the Rich Gritty Band!

Additional Resources

Dawn Lianna's Website: intuitivecallings.com

- ***8 Keys to Powerful Intuition E-Course with Audios***
- *Numerous Mp3 Files on developing your intuition and connecting with Angels and Spirit Guides*
- *Free articles, blog posts and newsletters*
- *Intuitive/ Psychic readings by phone internationally*

E-Courses at Daily Om

- *A Year of Angels in Your Inbox*
  #1 Best Seller!
- *Contact Your Angels for Empowerment*
- *Bring on Miracles with the Archangels*
- *Use Feng Shui to Create Greater Wealth*
- *Develop Powerful Intuition Ecourse*

Website: dailyom.com

Dawn Lianna's Best Selling University E-Course

Keys to Effective Communication

Website: ed2go.com

Additional Books By Dawn Lianna, M.A.

- *The Eight Keys to Powerful Intuition*
- *Angels Messages*
- *Chocolate Covered Dreams*
- *Lao Tzu Now by Lao Tzu and Dawn Lianna*
- *Tao Te Ching, The Art of Happiness by Lao Tzu and Dawn Lianna*

Dawn's International Trainings

- *Develop Powerful Intuition, Beg. Int. & Adv.*
- *The 8 Keys to Powerful Intuition*
- *Cracking the Prosperity Code*
- *Develop a Powerful Core Belief System*
- *Contact Your Guides and Angels for Empowerment, Beg. Int. and Adv.*
- *Vision Quest*
- *Topics also Taught by Teleseminar or Webinar*

Contact Dawn Lianna, M.A.

Dawn Lianna MA offers intuitive readings and intuition development training internationally. Please contact Dawn for a reading, to be introduced to your Guide Team or Angels, and if you want to host training in your area.

For trainings, phone readings, or sponsor a training in your area, contact Dawn Lianna.

503-699-3035

dawnlia@ yahoo.com

intuitivecallings.com

Do You Have an Angel Story?

I am accepting submissions for my next book and blog posts. If you would like to share a positive, loving story about an experience with an Angel or Guide, please email me your story at dawnlia@yahoo.com.

Love to you,

Dawn Lianna, M.A.

Made in the USA
Charleston, SC
23 November 2013